THE W

TOP 100

WAYS TO

CLOSE A SALE

In Pursuit Of Excellence

Crawley Priory
South Pallant
Chichester
PO19 1SY

Email: tonyhaywardassoc@fsmail.net

Published by Hayward Publishing

TONY HAYWARD

Tony Hayward in his chosen profession is probably the world's most experienced salesman. During the last 20 years he has visited and advised over 2,000 companies on their sales operations. Over 100,000 salespeople have attended his seminars. Much of his work is carried out at the sharp end showing eager salespeople how to close a sale.

Born and educated in Birmingham Tony now lives with his family in Chichester, England.

As an eighteen year old he started his career by selling vacuum cleaners door to door in Birmingham and finished up breaking a world record for Rolls Royce sales in Hong Kong.

Tony has worked in the United Kingdom, Bahamas, Bermuda, United States, Hong Kong, Saudi Arabia, Singapore and Europe and is convinced that selling skills, and in particular closing techniques, are universal.

After 20 years as an international salesman Tony founded Tony Hayward Associates in 1980 as a business to help coach salespeople world-wide to improve their skills and closing ratios. Currently 17 of the UK's top 20 profitable companies in his chosen field have used his services to develop their businesses. Tony has always stated "One closer is worth five order takers".

Published October 2003

Further information or more copies can be obtained from:
Hayward Publishing
Crawley Priory
South Pallant
Chichester
PO19 1SY

ISBN 0-9546198-0-3

Printed by: Selsey Press Ltd, 84 High Street, Selsey, Chichester, West Sussex PO20 0QH Tel: 01243 605234

CONTENTS

No. 21 - Price you won't go to close.

No. 22 - Client's story close.

No. 23 - Was it me close.

No. 24 - It is cheaper elsewhere close.

No. 25 - I cannot wait for delivery close.

No. 26 - Alternative close.

No. 27 - It is not in this year's budget close.

No. 28 - In terms of percentage close.

No. 29 - Shut up close.

No. 30 - Subject to close.

No. 31 - Meet not beat close.

No. 32 - Feel - felt - found close.

No. 33 - Cash back close.

No. 34 - Millionaire close.

No. 35 - Balance sheet close.

No. 36 - Half-Nelson close.

No. 37 - Side-step close.

No. 38 - Toss the coin close.

No. 39 - Autograph close.

No. 40 - Commission close.

No. 41 - Reversal close.

No. 42 - I'm just looking close.

No. 43 - Store voucher close.

No. 44 - Bridging close.

No. 45 - Management close.

No. 46 - Credit card close.

No. 47 - No deposit close.

No. 48 - Demonstration close.

No. 49 - Consent close.

No. 50 - Constant question close.

No. 51 - Indecision close.

No. 52 - Benefits recap close.

No. 53 - Secondary question close.

No. 54 - Qualification close.

No. 55 - Market edge close.

No. 56 - Motive close.

No. 57 - Second best close.

No. 58 - Personal reward close.

No. 59 - Empathy close.

No. 60 - Negotiation close.

No. 61 - I'll think about it close.

No. 62 - Box of chocs close.

No. 63 - Top drawer close.

No. 64 - Trial close.

No. 65 - Yes close.

No. 66 - Delivery close.

No. 67 - Let's pretend it's tomorrow close.

No. 68 - End user close.

No. 69 - Puppy dog close.

No. 70 - Finance close.

No. 71 - What is your best price close.

No. 72 - Sell what they want close.

No. 73 - Time limit close.

No. 74 - Order form close.

No. 75 - Plea close.

No. 76 -Hot potato close.

No. 77 - Inferior product close.

No. 78 - Upgrade close.

No. 79 - Lost memory close.

No. 80 - Multiple payment close.

No. 81 - Thank you for your offer close.

No. 82 - Hot coffee close.

No. 83 - Buyers remorse close.

No. 84 - Rejection close.

No. 85 - Margin share close.

No. 86 - Compete close.

No. 87 - Comparison close.

No. 88 - Discount v service close.

No. 89 - Breaktime close.

No. 90 - Resale value close.

No. 91 - Credit note close.

No. 92 - Payment saving close.

No. 93 - Sell yourself close.

No. 94 - Do not close.

No. 95 - Two up and one down close.

No. 96 - Extended monthly payments close.

No. 97 - Percentage of market close.

No. 98 - Piece of cake close.

No. 99 - Price justification close.

No. 100 -Thank you card close.

INTRODUCTION

I believe in teaching you can only take people as far as you have been yourself so having some 20,000 significant sales to date gives me some credence to write this book.

In this book of the top 100 closing skills you will read of many ideas you have not yet experimented with and I urge you to try them on your prospects and clients.

Selling is a changing market as we move into more advanced technology and product but one thing remains the same - we have to 'close the sale' or somebody else will.

If you have just started out in a selling career you cannot afford to have a negative, cynical, apathetic or unenthusiastic view to learning. If you have you would be better off having a duvet day than going to work.

Closing is 80% attitude and only 20% aptitude so you must have the confidence to ask for the order. Knowledge instils confidence, confidence instils enthusiasm and enthusiasm sells! Only 2% of people are self-motivated, 23% need supervision and 75% need a boss! So if one of your managers gives you advice on how to close - listen!

It has been said many times that selling is the most exciting thing you can do with your clothes on and is most certainly the best paid hard work and worst paid easy work you can find.

Remember too that you do not have to like people you sell to - getting them to like you is the way the game is played. Probably the most important psychological need of your buyer is to feel important. I expect you can think of many places you will not revisit to spend money where you were not treated with courtesy and recognition.

Selling is fun, and I am a fun person and would never have taken it up as a career if I was not going to enjoy myself at some stage every day. Closing is fun-inducing.

I always say to my delegates at conferences that the first 20 words you speak to someone are more important than the next 20,000. I recently met a salesman who was stuck for an answer when I said "good morning". Listen to people and identify their needs correctly and use the words "both of you" many times when dealing with two people. It is important to learn the skill of answering a question with a question because the person who asks questions and listens is in control. A chairman of a large company asked me recently over lunch why I always answered a question with question to which I replied "Why not?"

In closing you will only attempt what your fear will permit and that is why so many sales are lost - simply because the salesperson was too fearful to ask for the business.

To learn 100 ways to close a sale has taken me a lifetime of learning but this is your opportunity to store that knowledge which will undoubtedly give you the financial rewards you plan for. When your opportunity knocks don't complain about the noise!

This is a unique opportunity for you to vastly increase your lifestyle. By choosing to read this book is a testament to your own good judgement.

Points to Note

My definition of closing is "To provide face-savers to prospects and clients who have usually asked for too much in the transaction".

Many salespeople fail to close because they have a fear of rejection so take the easy way out. If you never want to fail at the closing stage the answer is simple "Don't ask for the order!" I once asked a salesman to go back to his client and ask for another £100 profit to which the salesman replied he was afraid of losing the deal. My answer was "You cannot lose what you haven't got!" Fifteen years later and now a successful company sales director he still remembers that moment.

In general as salespeople you are paid on production by way of commission. It is no good walking around with an order book of "Nearly sold labels" and your manager will tell you that you cannot invoice good enquiries. If you are paid to sell by your company but you are failing to close it means you are making money for the competition - which usually ends up with you in the departure lounge awaiting the short exit interview of maybe two or three chosen words.

If you have a conversion rate of two out of every ten people you try to close, ask yourself how many closes do you know. Remarkably if you go from 2/10 to 3/10 you have a 50% increase in profit. 100 closes will help you to achieve that greater income for your family.

Many salespeople are obviously disappointed when an order is cancelled. My many years of experience tells me that the top salespeople will attract more cancelled transactions than an order taker because they are always closing. If the client likes and respects you it is sometimes difficult for them to say "No" face to face so have to go away and write you a letter. Bottom line is though that you will end up with more sales at the year end because of your persistence.

Note it is also more difficult for the buyer to close than yourself because in most cases you have the training and knowledge behind you. What the prospect or client expects from you is for you to make it easy by your choice of words, sentences and alternatives.

Winners buy - losers walk were the words my manager said to me every day when I was learning my trade. If people have hope to gain and fear of loss in a purchase you need to show them the benefits of their decision to buy.

Closing a sale is a sharp end skill and those who are paid to do so are admired by top management and subordinates when successful. It is not just salespeople who have to possess this skill but the C.E.O., Chairman, Managing Director and most line managers have to master it.

Avoid negotiating a close if possible at the time of day when you are not at your best! Make appointments that suit your character. Are you better in the morning, afternoon or evening? I am writing this book between 7.00 am and 12 noon most days because I know my brain is sharper. When possible all my business appointments are made to suit me so that my negotiation skills are stronger.

Always indicate that each concession you give is a loss to you and your company. If appropriate it is okay to use humour but do not take risks in this area even if you feel you know the client well enough.

God gave us two ears and one mouth so he must have been trying to tell us something - maybe listen more than we talk.

We only learn by listening, watching and doing, all things to bear in mind when negotiating. If you listen you may find that the prospect's desires are closer to yours than you expect. Always be willing to adjust your position if you can see a close early in the proceedings. Make your first offer unrealistic and go forward from that point - winners buy! Any offers the client makes take note of to show that you take them seriously.

There are three major ways to close a sale:

1. By mail (including fax, email, etc.)

2. By telephone.

3. By face to face.

Most top salespeople use all three methods in their selling process. You will need to decide which is your best bet for maximum results.

N.B. Each of the 100 closing skills I am now going to put to you are in no order of importance. Each buyer is different as is each selling situation. I urge you to study them and guarantee an increase in your income if you practice what you learn.

NO. 1

I'VE HAD A BETTER OFFER CLOSE

When you make an offer to a buyer in more cases than not they say those magical words "I've had a better offer!" To my amazement I have heard salespeople of many years' experience say things such as:

"What was the offer?"

or

"How far apart are we?"

or

"What have we got to beat?"

Now unless I am very mistaken, do not most people hide behind those words to get a better deal and will exaggerate the truth somewhat if asked for a figure. Once they mention a figure they have been offered how can they accept less without appearing to be a liar?

I once had a man of the cloth tell me he had a better offer to which I looked up to the heavens and said "Do you think your boss pointed you in the wrong direction this morning?" He did eventually buy after some fierce negotiation. To deal with this type of objection you need to ask the following questions:

A. "When was the offer?"

"Was it today?"

"Was it yesterday?"

"Was it this week?"

"Was it last week?"

"Was it this month?"

"Was it last month?"

"Was it during the last three months?"

You may be able to point out that the offer may not now be valid!

B. "Where was the offer?"

"Was it local?"

"Was it a competitor?"

"Was it in another town or city?"

"Was it under limited special offer?"

If the offer was some way away you may be able to point out that they may incur a delivery charge!

C. "Were the goods/article in stock?"

Many companies quote low figures when no stock! To order may cost extra! Did they quote delivery charges?

D. "Were the goods/article a current model?"

Beware of old stock being moved on at a reduced price.

E. "Have you got the offer in writing?"

Remember a verbal quote can be exaggerated! An unwritten quote may not be an official offer. Was it management approved?

Remember your credibility may be damaged if you respond too fast to the other party's figures. Information should be exchanged and questions asked constantly. Use delaying methods if you do not want to respond to their offer immediately. Break off the negotiations to liaise with your manager or colleagues especially if they know you have to refer the figures.

To close this sale you have to consider:

1. Do you compete with any written offer.
2. Do you believe any verbal quote.
3. If you think the offer may not be real, use delivery, stock, finance rates if appropriate and after-sales customer care to gain the business.

<u>CLOSE THE SALE</u>

NO. 2

FUNNY MONEY CLOSE

Buyers are looking for your best price.

N.B.

A. £6,000 is not your best first offer.

B. £150 discount is not your best first offer.

People have to believe that you have looked at your cost price and have calculated the best offer you can. I am amazed in so many dealing situations where people round off the figures thinking the buyer will accept!

To negotiate both parties need to relate to the figures in question. What you want is a mutually agreeable outcome incorporating the winners buy - losers walk philosophy. If you dive in at the deep end with your best offer it is likely that they will be pushed into a take it or leave it situation and the negotiations will fail. If you both agree that negotiations may be necessary, then your chances of success are much greater. Do not make your presentation of figures too rigid. Ask questions and then listen.

Do not start speaking until you have something relevant to say. If you agree to an offer in haste you must repent at leisure. Look the buyer in the face when making your offer.

A funny money close is:

£6,137.50 - not £6,000.

£142.50 discount - not £150.

This will appear as your best price to the buyer!

N.B. Round up the figures if necessary to conclude

CLOSE THE SALE

NO. 3

BODY LANGUAGE CLOSE

How you appear to your prospect is of paramount importance. You do not get a second chance to get it right first time. Power dressing can influence in certain types of meetings but it can also appear aggressive to certain people. If in doubt dress conservatively. Beware of cultural differences. After working in Asia I am well aware that physical contact between opposite sexes is discouraged and consideration should be given as to whether you shake hands.

Eyes are the most expressive part of the body and can reveal whether a close is imminent. Contact with another person's eyes indicates that you want to give or receive information. Be alert to this as the signal you get may only last a fleeting moment.

Let me list some of the positive and negative body language signals you may receive at the closing stage.

Nodding of the head - positive. **N.B.** - in Bulgaria it means disagreement.

Shaking the head - negative. **N.B.** - in Bulgaria it is positive.

Smiling - positive. **N.B.** - in Korea it indicates too pushy.

Leaning back - implies hostility.

Crossed arms - indicates disbelief.

Leaning forward - shows paying attention.

Open hands - open mind.

Unbuttoned coat - open mind.

Hand on chin - shows thoughtfulness.

Inattentive gaze - means lack of concentration.

Fiddling with pencil - confirms thoughts are elsewhere.

Open arms - imply indecision.

Wide eyes - indicates willingness to be persuaded.

Steepling fingers - authoritative gesture.

Hands on back of head - showing confidence.

Hands in coat pockets, thumbs outside - authoritative gesture.

Hands in your pockets - he is after your wallet - just checking!

Raised eyebrows - shows irritation.

Tilted head - undecided or boredom.

Touching ear - not convinced what they are hearing.

Crossing legs - defensive.

Clenching fists - wary of your proposal.

Stroking chin - thinking about it.

Taking off glasses to clean - unsure.

Clearing throat - nervous.

Lighting a cigarette - positive, go for close.

Putting cigarette out on back of your hand - lost sale - just checking!

Tugging at ear - unsure.

Making tutting sound - irritable.

Rubbing back of neck - annoyance.

Doodling - bored.

Drumming fingers - not bought - resell. Create desire.

Rubbing palms - thinking of money and proposal.

Jingling money - expects to do business.

Nodding - go for close - unless in Bulgaria!

Handshake - You have closed the sale.

CLOSE THE SALE

NO. 4

FEAR CLOSE

As mentioned earlier, buyers have a hope to gain - fear of loss attitude when making a purchase.

What are the fears that people have when they sit down to consider your product?

1. Fear that you are not a person of integrity.
2. Fear that you are not the best supplier.
3. Fear that they won't get value for money.
4. Fear that their present product is not working.
5. Fear that you will not have the product in stock.
6. Fear that you may not have the correct model/colour.
7. Fear that they may not be accepted on credit.
8. Fear of a price increase if they are hesitant.
9. Fear of a price reduction if they wait.
10. Fear of failing to negotiate an acceptable price.
11. Fear of debt.
12. Fear of losing face with family and friends.
13. Fear of past experiences when purchasing.
14. Fear generated by "knowledgeable friends".
15. Fear that delivery will not be soon enough!

The above are just a few of the fears people have when buying your product. By listening carefully to the other party and leaving enough room to manoeuvre your figures you can overcome these fears.

By indicating that you have limited stock/limited colour choice/other parties interested in that product/a hint of manufacturer's price rises can all help to convince the purchaser.

CLOSE THE SALE

NO. 5

REDUCTION CLOSE

A reduction close is where you reduce the balance apart downwards to an acceptable level for your buyer.

Negotiating can be a painful process for both you and your customer. Anxiety over the result because it is some time since you made a sale does not help. You may feel worried that they are going to walk away. Remember a sale is made not won. Prospects should be persuaded that they will benefit from saying yes to your proposition. Listen to a person's tone of voice not just their words. If they are speaking slowly and deliberately it will indicate they are comfortable in your company. If they smile unnecessarily and start speaking more quickly can indicate nervousness. Note that people who want to leave tend to look and turn their bodies towards the exit.

Examples of the reduction closes are:

A. If you are £700 apart on price ask how long they will keep it on purchase. i.e. £700 over 5 years is 38 pence per day and you cannot even buy a newspaper for that.

B. If the cost is £50 a month over their budget point out that is £1.66 per day so they are the price of a sandwich away from owning your product.

CLOSE THE SALE

IF YOU WAIT TOO LONG TO ASK THE QUESTION YOU ARE AVOIDING IT!

NO. 6

COMMITMENT CLOSE

This is universally known as the "If I can - will you" close and is probably the most used skill especially where a management or third party referral is necessary. Usually this situation occurs when the buyer asks for something in the transaction such as:

1. A price.
2. A delivery date.
3. An accessory.
4. An extra guarantee.

When you hear the other person's request do not feel that you have to respond instantly with a counter-offer. Stay as calm as you can and repeat the request to the buyer to show you have completely understood their words. At this time home in on any issues that you are unsure of.

If you feel sure that you are in a position to meet their request try to do so using third party skills. For example, say you will need to contact your manager by mobile for approval, or go to the office if on the premises.

Having gained third party approval to the figures then ask the question.

Example: "If I can obtain that colour at the agreed figure, will you okay the paperwork today?"

CLOSE THE SALE

NO. 7

FINAL OFFER CLOSE

This close is to be used when you are about to present your final proposal. When you are near this concluding moment, beware of a false declaration.

At an earlier moment in the negotiations you may have felt the need to say this was your best price. Whilst this is common practice be very careful not to state this is your final offer when you know it is not. This can lose your credibility when you suddenly come forward with a "final-final offer". Always prepare how and when you bring in your top price and make it clear that as much as you want their business you cannot move any further in the negotiations.

Present your final offer by your choice of words, tone of voice and body language. Create an atmosphere of decisiveness and increase the urgency and firmness in your voice. If you are not satisfied with the deal, do not sign it.

Examples:

1. "I have management instructions to state that this is our final offer."

2. "This is my "final offer", I have no margin to go any further."

3. "I have exceeded the figure my supervisor has given me re discount."

4. "This figure is our final offer. Let us complete the paperwork while the manager is still on the premises to authorise it."

CLOSE THE SALE

NO. 8

CONCESSIONS CLOSE

To close some people you will from time to time have to make certain concessions. It may be that you have to add accessories free of charge, upgrade the model they are buying or guarantee an earlier delivery date. Discount, it should always be remembered, is also a concession.

Having chosen your method of closing, prepare to ask the persuasive questions. Be aware of any mood swings by the buyer and try to present your offer at an upbeat stage in the conversation. This can make the difference between success and failure. Make sure that the person you are talking to has full authority to close the sale.

When you make an offer that involves a concession make sure it fits into their buying motive and game plan. Try to come to a conclusion without jeopardising your company's profit targets or reputation.

A concession as part of your sales process at the closing stage can break any deadlock. Whilst remembering winners buy - losers walk, you have to be careful when your buyer tries to gain even more concessions.

If you make them too late in the negotiations this sometimes can undermine your credibility. They sometimes wonder why you waited so long to present these into the deal.

Present your concession prior to your final close.

<u>CLOSE THE SALE</u>

NO. 9

TWO TO ONE CLOSE

When you are dealing with two people such as a married couple, partners etc., this close must be considered if you want to conclude the sale.

If you are sitting opposite two people and trying to close the sale one thing is for sure, no way will they both mentally decide to go ahead at your price. Your advantage is that generally they are both looking at you and not at each other. If you are observant to body language you will notice when one person seems agreeable enough to go for the close.

A lot of salespeople, if recognising this buying signal, then make the mistake of switching their attention to the uncommitted partner. This can cause conflict as they dig their heels in and sometimes leads to a change of mind of the 'already sold' partner.

I mentioned in my introduction the importance of using the words "both of you" as much as possible in your qualification and presentation. One partner tends to take the lead in the negotiations but the quieter person may be the major influence.

Example

Look the committed person in the eye and say that it is now decision time. Recap on the benefits and ask if they are happy so far. On receiving their approval state that you also believe it is the right decision. Turn to the other party and say "that is two out of three - what do you think?"

CLOSE THE SALE

NO. 10

SHARP ANGLE CLOSE

Buyers are sometimes very adept at persuading you to agree to a condition so that you are committed. Danger of this though is you also need agreement from the buyer.

Example

"If I chose two of those computers could you have them delivered and installed into my business by the end of this month?"

Should you agree they can say "Okay, I will let you know in the next few days!" - No sale!

One of the difficult things about new sales techniques and learning in general is that we are all creatures of habit and change is difficult. Every morning when you put your pants on you put the same leg in first - tomorrow morning try putting your other leg in first. When you have picked yourself up off the floor you will understand my meaning. Loss of sales and personal career damage which can be caused through lack of knowledge and ignorance can be so devastating that some people give up the selling profession altogether.

A correct way to answer the buyer's statement above is: "If I can guarantee, in writing, delivery and installation by the end of the month, would you okay the paperwork today?"

That is a sharp angle close - gaining commitment in reply to the buyer's attempt to commit you!

CLOSE THE SALE

IN CLOSING YOU CANNOT SOLVE PROBLEMS
UNLESS YOU ARE AWARE OF THEM!

NO. 11

ECONOMY CLOSE

If you are selling motor cars, motorcycles, motor boats, vans or trucks this close can be very effective. It also works in any industry where you can point out a cost saving element to convince the buyer to go ahead. If you are selling heating, electrical goods, double glazing or household running costs it can be usefully employed. Many other industries also employ this skill.

Example

"At the moment, Mr. Jones, we are £600 away from your price to upgrade your car. If I could bridge that gap and find £600 from somewhere would you be happy to go ahead with the order?"

If yes, continue: "At the present time your car does 32 mpg while the government quoted figure on this model is 39 mpg. At present you are driving some 15,000 miles per annum with a fuel cost of around £3.86 per gallon. Over three years this will give you a saving of £974.28 at today's fuel prices. In addition to the £600 difference you still come out with £374.28 saving in a three year period. Your pen or mine?"

Of course you need to work these figures out with a calculator or computer in front of your buyer but figures do not lie.

As mentioned, this cost saving method to bridge price differences is a very useful tool which I have used many, many times.

CLOSE THE SALE

NO. 12

VEHICLE KEY CLOSE

This is a control method to help you close the sale and introduce a third party or manager into the negotiations. It is only valid when the buyer visits your premises in a vehicle.

You ask the buyer if they have parked on your premises and suggest that the keys are kept in the manager's office in case it has to be moved due to congestion, etc! This you say will enable you to present your product without interruption.

Once you have this control there is no way that they can leave during the middle of your discussions. If they reject your first proposal or you are finding difficulty in concluding the sale you still have control.

It gives you the opportunity when they wish to leave to discuss your dilemma with a third party/manager who can then return the keys and try to assist the sale. Those people selling cars or motorbikes etc. find this a particularly useful closing tool.

The extra time that this allows you increases the likelihood of your proposal being given proper consideration.

It is a great pity that good salespeople who have the ability to become great salespeople never take off because they think they know it all and excuse themselves from the learning process. If you want to earn more, learn more.

CLOSE THE SALE

NO. 13

ASSUMPTIVE CLOSE

An assumptive close is when you assume the buyer is going to purchase your product.

This method is best used with personal friends, relatives, neighbours, previous clients and also return visit prospects.

It is not advisable to be assumptive with strangers, first time buyers, etc. who know nothing about you or your company.

When you know your buyer on a personal basis they can relax with you. It is very hard for strangers who are about to spend money to feel this way as it is in most cases a decision making process. Your friends, family and previous customers like you and trust you and that is why they have a face to face situation with you.

For much of the time these people will be easy to read. That is because they have dealt with you before or are related. They will be reactive to your comments and actions and will respond when necessary. You expect them to be open and cordial and they expect you to be friendly and polite. Do not let yourself down with body language and be aware of theirs.

Now that you both know each other and have smiled and greeted each other you can close very quickly on assumptive statements.

Example

"As I said, Richard, the asking price on the machine is reduced to £493 and I can deliver it to Sarah and yourself on Tuesday or Thursday. Which is best for you?"

CLOSE THE SALE

NO. 14

NODDING CLOSE

I have already indicated the importance of body language. It is now time for me to go into more depth about the nodding close.

It is said that 15% of the population are 'natural nodders', i.e. people who, when they are thinking positive and agreeable thoughts, will nod their heads.

During your qualification questions it will be relatively easy for you to establish whether you are dealing with a person with such inclinations. If you find yourself dealing with this kind of buyer it is best to follow this procedure when executing the close.

Prior to your proposal, ask them two questions that, firstly they will know the answer to and, secondly, will answer with a yes. Then present your figures.

<u>Example</u>

"Mrs. Jackson, can I just confirm a couple of things with you before we discuss price?" (Yes - nod). "You work for A.B.C. Solicitors in Birmingham city centre, correct?" (yes - nod), "and you say that this laptop will be of great use to your everyday life with the company going to reimburse 50% of the value - am I right?" (Yes - nod).

Now you look Mrs. Jackson between the eyes and slowly start to <u>nod your head</u> with the following statement: "Mrs. Jackson, having looked at the figures the very best price we can offer you while stock is available is £932.47. I am sure you will agree that is fair and reasonable, don't you agree?" <u>Yes - nod</u>!

By asking 'nodding' questions and then executing the close in a joint 'nodding' scenario you will find a conclusion simple.

<u>CLOSE THE SALE</u>

NO. 15

REFERRAL CLOSE

I want to relay to you a very simple and obvious fact. If you gain one referral deal from everyone you sell to, you double your income. Correct or not correct?

When a buyer pays for their product they like you, trust in you and are more than happy with their purchase.

During the next few days, weeks and months they will be showing people their new acquisition. This is the time they should be recommending their friends or family to visit you for a similar purchase.

Ensure that you and your company, along with the product, are beyond reproach because bad publicity spreads faster than good. Satisfied clients will tell about five/ten people about their buying experience with you. A disgruntled client will probably tell 50 or as many as will listen. An old saying in selling is 'Don't fan the flames of discontented customers'. You do not want to wave goodbye to all the fantastic business opportunities that can come your way.

Example

"Before I hand over this product to you I would like to say what a pleasure it has been to do business with you. I now feel that half of my job is done. When someone comes to me and purchases because of your recommendation I will feel I have done my job correctly. Do you know of any friends, family or colleagues whom I might contact in the near future?"

A financial reward is always useful!

CLOSE THE SALE

CLOSING IS NUTRITION TO A SALESPERSON

TAKE IT DAILY IN LARGE DOSES!

NO. 16

'ADDITIONAL HELP' CLOSE

A little unasked for help can many times convince the buyer that you have their interests at heart. Let me give you an excellent example of this.

Andrew is a sales manager who I have worked with for the last twelve months. He works in a car dealership in the north of England. We have exchanged tips, closes and ideas on frequent occasions since we met. Andrew was a late starter in the motor trade but will rapidly rise within the industry because of his hard work and open mind. How is the Atkins diet, Andrew?

Whilst working in their very busy showroom one day I observed an elderly lady carrying two heavy shopping bags looking longingly at a small car on their used car display. On talking to her she stated she had written her own car off six months previously which had unnerved her with regard to driving. She had tried to manage by public transport but was finding that very tiresome.

I took her shopping bags from her and led her into Andrew's office to explain the dilemma. Andrew sat her down with a cup of coffee and listened to her tale of woe. He then took her out in the car, driving himself to show her the benefits. Of course no trade-in was involved and a good margin was in the vehicle. Instead of mentioning discount Andrew said "I will pay for a driving school at our expense to take you out to boost your confidence.

She bought.

CLOSE THE SALE

NO. 17

HANDSHAKE CLOSE

When you conclude a sale it usually means someone has handed over a credit card or cash in a retail shop situation. With more expensive items and certainly those where credit is involved then paperwork has to be signed. I try to avoid the word contract as much as possible as it is a rejection word in our industry. Sure thing is though pen has to be put to paper.

I have seen many salespeople over the years sitting at their desks face to face with prospects and afraid to ask for the order. These people who have the habit of extending the selling scenario long past its sell by date should learn to close with a handshake.

My estimation is that 80% of all people who shake hands on an agreement will then sit down to finalise details. Now there are a good couple of words - finalise details. Does not that sound better than saying filling in the order form or signing the contract. No wonder some salespeople have a brown haemorrhage when it comes to the close - it is because they have not learned the right words or actions to take.

On completion of your presentation and proposals you stand smartly up from your chair (hopefully the buyer may still be sitting down), look them firmly in the eye and extend your right arm in the direction of their right hand. Say something like, "A handshake confirms my commitment to treating you as a valued customer, thank you for your business!"

Make sure your hands are clean.

CLOSE THE SALE

NO. 18

COST PLUS CLOSE

When you are negotiating with a business person who is in wholesale or retail this close may be of use to you.

In many businesses and industries companies sell goods with a mark up of anything between 50% and 300%. If you are working in much smaller percentages be wary of how you present your proposal. If you say that you will give 8% discount to buyers who mark their goods up by 200% it will not be impressive. You may yourself be working with a 15% margin and quite happy to give 8% away. Having qualified the buyer correctly with the cost plus close you would say something like this.

"Mrs. Stubbs, I do enjoy talking with local business people because they understand what retained margins are necessary to run a company. We have at the moment a special offer for local businesses such as yours. We can offer today the product at 7% over cost. I will show you our cost price so there is no misunderstanding. Would you be looking at delivery this month or next?"

Showing people, with written proof, a margin that they would not be able to work with in their own business puts you on the road to a sale. When the time is right, and the buyer is in wholesale or retail use cost plus and not discount off.

CLOSE THE SALE

NO. 19

VERBAL REMINDER CLOSE

This close is to be used as a benefit recap in selling situations where your qualification, presentation and demonstration may have been over some period of time in hours, days or even weeks.

Once you have placed yourself in a position to close you remind them of all the benefits.

Example

"Let me just recap on some of the benefits before we talk price:

1. We have the car in stock.
2. It is the colour both you and your wife favour.
3. It is the current model.
4. Your wife was very comfortable in the car.
5. Your children were as safe as if they were in Fort Knox.
6. The economy is much better than your current model.
7. Interest rates on finance are at their lowest.

Now have you anything whatsoever that you wish to discuss before we talk price?"

By going over and reminding the buyer of all the benefits, you should have created the desire for him to snap your hand off when you offer your proposal.

Do not make it sound like a monologue, as if you have said the same thing 100 times this week. Make an extra effort to customise your benefits. You will then appear confident, sincere and knowledgeable about your buyer's wants and needs.

Remember when people go out to buy a chosen product all they are looking for is a salesperson.

CLOSE THE SALE

NO. 20

"WE WILL LET YOU KNOW TOMORROW" CLOSE

When your buyer attempts to break off the negotiations with you they say things such as "I'll think about it", "I'll let you know" or sometimes a more positive "We will let you know tomorrow". However what you have to establish is do they or do they not want to buy the product.

My immediate response to "We will let you know tomorrow" is, "No problem, would you like me to put a 'reserved' sticker on the machine until you contact me tomorrow?"

If the answer is "No, if it goes, it goes" it means you have failed to sell and you need to re-qualify and present the benefits in more detail.

If the answer is "Yes, if you could!" it means you have failed to close. This person must be closed today and my approach was always "I am sure it is no problem but I will go and check with my senior manager". When returning shortly afterwards I said "I do have good news and not so good news. Firstly I can hold the machine in reserve for you but the not so good news is this. One of our sales team has also someone interested in the same machine and he is calling in at 6.00 p.m. tonight. I am instructed that I can reserve it but only until 5.00 p.m. It is now 3.15 p.m. which gives you 1 hour 45 minutes. Would that be enough? Of course at the moment you can solve the problem by approving the sale as you are first in line. So many of my clients have been disappointed by an initial action of hesitancy!"

CLOSE THE SALE

BUYERS NEED YOUR ADVICE

NO. 21

PRICE YOU WON'T GO TO CLOSE

One of the most annoying scenarios in selling is this.

Buyers state that they are visiting two companies for a price on exactly the same product. They add that they will deal with the best offer and you are the first company to be visited.

Now these type of people are very difficult to conclude on their first visit because of the up-front statement they have made.

Of course some salespeople will say "Come back and see me when you have a price and I am sure I can beat it"; only the buyer knows quite well that this is just sales talk. My way of dealing with this was by using the 'price you won't go to' close.

Firstly I would advise them that I would phone my manager/head office for a competitive price. I would sell myself and all the back-up customer care we offer and also say, "I cannot remember the last deal we lost on price".

Now is the important bit! I then quote a figure that my head office have told me I cannot go to. This price would be way out of the reach of any competitor. I would then say, "If you are offered this figure at the other company, take it because we cannot deliver at that price. If they do not offer that price come back and we will help in any way we can". Guess what! Most of them come back without an offer for me to accommodate!

CLOSE THE SALE

NO. 22

CLIENT'S STORY CLOSE

By talking about the advantages one of your clients gained after purchasing your product can be a useful closing tool.

You may, for instance, be selling a couple the benefits of a payment protection plan on a loan they have taken on your goods.

"Sarah, Steve, I know you have a few doubts about the extra cost of the protection plan with a growing family like yours. I did in fact talk to a couple of clients with similar commitments under a year ago. They decided to go for the plan, after some earlier reservations, on a van they bought.

Only five months later James had a car accident and has been off work ever since with a back problem. They both have found that the payment protection is actually a ray of sunshine when everything else around them is very gloomy.

James's wife said that they have been able to keep the van as she now has to drive the children to and from school and other activities. Yes I think the few pence a day protection has served them well during this trying time!

We all want peace of mind when it comes to investing money, don't we? Who can guarantee what will happen to their jobs or health over the next few years.

Would you prefer two or three year protection?"

CLOSE THE SALE

NO. 23

"WAS IT ME?" CLOSE

Over 100,000 salespeople have attended my 'Close that Sale' seminars. During my presentations I tell them that we must always give a professional image of our industry. I have explained that you will always give good images if you give your customers a thoroughly professional service.

As a salesperson I was successful because I am, above all else, 'a people's person'. Nobody can sell to everybody but I wanted those who had decided not to buy my product still to be glad that they met me. I cannot ever remember selling a customer something they did not want or need. To overcome people's fear of loss I always portrayed a hope to gain.

"Was it me?" close is an exaggerated plea close and is to be used when you have tried everything and they still will not put pen to paper. If you are in their office what you say is something like this.

"Just before I go, Mr. Williams, can I apologise for not being successful today. I believe that I have obviously failed to show you the benefit of our product. Now you and your company will not be able to reap the rewards our product and service offer. I naturally believe in my product and support my family by helping clients own it. So I don't go down the wrong road again, Mr. Williams, can you spare me a couple of minutes to tell me what I did wrong?"

CLOSE THE SALE

NO. 24

IT IS CHEAPER ELSEWHERE CLOSE

When you are trying to sell a product how many times do you hear people say "It is cheaper elsewhere"? It is something the buyer wants to believe and you must always be ready to hear it and close accordingly.

You must explain to them how long you have been in business and what you have learned to understand. Tell them people look for three things if they are spending money, quality, service and the cheapest price. Explain that no company can offer all three. Ask them which they would be prepared to negotiate on, quality, after-sales service or price. It is usually difficult for your buyer to come back at you and accept poor quality or poor service. So it is now left for you to close on your price.

Here is an alternative example which you may prefer.

Client: "Tony, I am sure I have seen products like this at a much cheaper price."

You: "Ronald, I could have chosen to work with any distributor in this area. After carefully looking at my options I chose this company because I could tell my clients, with integrity, that they were dealing with a company that not only promises, but also delivers, top quality goods. Those few extra pounds per week are an investment for you to benefit from in the long term and have my personal attention. Fair and reasonable, isn't it?"

CLOSE THE SALE

NO. 25

I CANNOT WAIT FOR DELIVERY CLOSE

Overcoming objections, turning them into stepping stones is the only way to conclude the sale. Listed below are some common objections we have to deal with.

1. OBJECTION — "It is too dear!"

   Turn into question — "What you are asking me, Miss Smythe, is how we can justify the price of this particular model?"

   Answer the question — By explaining - the value of the product to justify the price.

2. OBJECTION — "We are satisfied with our existing product."

   Turn into question — "What you want to know, Mr. Foster, is what makes this product better than your existing one?"

   Answer the question — By explaining - the benefits of features of your product against his.

3. OBJECTION — "We are satisfied with our existing supplier."

   Turn into question — "I see, so what you want to know is why there is a valid reason to buy from us that outweighs your current loyalties?"

	Answer the question	By explaining - the advantages of dealing with your company but without criticising their existing supplier.
4.	OBJECTION	"I haven't the time to talk to you."
	Turn into question	"What you are asking me is what you will gain by giving me some of your valuable time."
	Answer the question	By explaining - that you are not there to sell to them but to help them purchase without any immediate commitment on their part.
5.	OBJECTION	"I cannot wait for delivery - I want it now!"
	Turn into question	"What you want to know are the advantages to be gained by waiting."
	Answer the question	By explaining - that to rush delivery would put pressure on production and maybe only 98% quality. 100% of quality is worth waiting a short while for.
6.	OBJECTION	"I cannot afford to buy at the moment."
	Turn into question	"What you are asking is, is there any way in which we can help

you purchase now to avoid price increases."

Answer the question	By explaining - low cost finance - credit and charge card facility - monthly/weekly payments. How much more they will pay by waiting.

CLOSE THE SALE

ACHIEVEMENT DIFFERENTIATES BETWEEN
A CLOSER AND AN ORDER TAKER!

NO. 26

ALTERNATIVE CLOSE

An alternative close is where you give the buyer two, three or even four alternatives. An answer of yes to any of them means they have bought.

Examples

1. "Would you like delivery on Thursday afternoon or Friday morning?"
2. "We can deliver the carpet to your home on Monday at 9.00 am or would 3.00 pm be more convenient for you?"
3. "Will you be wanting the blue or deep red?"
4. "Monthly payments would be:

   1 year - £276.48 per month

   2 years - £149.31 per month

   3 years - £99.47 per month

   Which would you prefer?"
5. "You can take this cooker from display or I can order you one with around 14 days delivery - which are you happier with?"
6. "Would you prefer this model in manual or automatic?"
7. "Do you favour 1 year or 2 years extended warranty?"
8. "When would you like the critical illness policy to expire - 10 years or 20 years - the choice is yours?"

9. "Are you paying cash or by card?"

A few examples above which you can adapt to your own profession and products.

This is a very successful form of closing.

CLOSE THE SALE

NO. 27

"IT IS NOT IN THIS YEAR'S BUDGET" CLOSE

When making a presentation to a company buyer you are sometimes hit with the above statement. What you have to do is show value for money, cost saving, etc. and not walk away until next year. This ploy is used by people in business to deter "Mr. Average Salesperson".

You are a successful business person yourself and understand why budgets are planned and adhered to. You also know that on many occasions contingency plans are made if a need arises that adds value to the business in the short or long term.

Point out that you appreciate that financial controls have to be well managed but this should not deter them from listening to your proposal. Say that most budgets are flexible and as a valued employee or manager they must have authority to show their peers/colleagues that a certain product is in the best interest of the company's five year plan (i.e. pull them out of the current year budget thinking!).

Show examples that your product will not only produce a more competitive edge to their business but will in a short time cut costs. Point out that next year the product may not be so readily available and will most certainly be at a higher cost.

<u>CLOSE THE SALE</u>

NO. 28

IN TERMS OF PERCENTAGE CLOSE

Before you start to use your closing skills on a buyer you must know how much they want your product. Be flexible in your discussions - it is a sign of strength not weakness. Try to learn tactics from the biographies of famous negotiators.

If your buyer appears confused use visual aids to clarify issues that are creating the problem Put your complex figures down on paper using short clear sentences; be prepared to involve a third party to review the issues.

Should you have an aggressive buyer repeat all the facts, stay focused and avoid emotional conversation. Do not get drawn into heated argument. Provide refreshments in coffee, etc. to defuse the situation.

Sometimes your buyer may become emotional about the purchase but do not challenge their motives or integrity. Reply to emotional behaviour with rational questioning.

After you have demonstrated or presented your product to the buyer, ask the question:

"Now that you have seen this music centre with all its benefits and features, can I ask you a question - in terms of percentage how much would you like to own it for your home?"

If the answer is 85% or more say, "Anybody who wants a product that much I would feel I had let down if they did not walk away with it. Would you like delivery this week or later?"

CLOSE THE SALE

NO. 29

"SHUT UP" CLOSE

Otherwise known as the silence close this method is known by many and practised by such a small minority.

Many people outside our profession often say things like "He is a natural salesperson because he has the gift of the gab" or "She would make a great salesperson because she has an answer for everything".

If only these people knew that the biggest skill of all is knowing when to shut up. Power of silence is frightening when used at the right time.

Yesterday I was watching on TV a press conference with Sir Alex Ferguson, the manager of Manchester United Football Club. One eager reporter asked him a sensitive question about a reported confrontation with David Beckham in the dressing room. Sir Alex just looked him straight in the eye for around ten seconds and said absolutely nothing. An embarrassed reporter mumbled an apology to which Sir Alex said "next question".

When you have qualified your buyer's needs, been friendly and unfailingly polite, presented your product and arrived at the closing stage, remember the selling is finished.

When the closing starts, present your offer professionally and with conviction. Look your buyer in the eyes, reiterate your commitment to customer care and after sales and ask for the order!

Then shut up! First to speak is usually the loser.

CLOSE THE SALE

NO. 30

SUBJECT TO CLOSE

A subject to close is very useful where the buyer has made his mind up to purchase but maybe has a touch of buyer's remorse and gives one reason for making the decision the next day.

A subject to close is where you sign someone up and take a deposit subject to that condition.

I always say to salespeople when I am working with them at the 'sharp end': "Make sure you have the M.C." Now M.C. has nothing to do with master of ceremonies or M.C. Hammer the faded pop star. It means mental commitment. People will not pay for a product financially until they own it mentally.

Avoid a win/lose situation and point out that you are looking out for them. State that you do not want them to feel they have been forced into any decision but you also do not want them to lose the product by indecision. Avoid confrontation which will result in hostility and deadlock. Adopt a relaxed atmosphere so constructive discussion takes place.

Examples

"You can okay the paperwork subject to colour choice!"

"Go ahead subject to your partner's approval."

"We can reserve the goods subject to delivery date!"

"I will hold the boat for you subject to your conversation with the bank manager."

CLOSE THE SALE

CLOSING IS 10% PERSPIRATION

AND

90% INSPIRATION!

NO. 31

MEET NOT BEAT CLOSE

To use this close you need to be working with a product where other companies sell exactly the same models at the same recommended retail price.

When I am working in those situations I hear people give to sales people a price they have been offered elsewhere. It is rather disappointing for me to hear the employee answer:

"If I match the offer, will you go ahead?" or "What figure have I got to beat?"

It is very often that a buyer will inflate his asking price to negotiate a better deal. I always believe a prospect has 1) an asking price, 2) a liking price, and 3) a taking price. Should you agree to match or beat an offer you may be turning the buyer into a serial shopper. They will think the more they 'shop around' the better price they will obtain.

When given a price by the prospect always agree that that is an exceptional offer which would be hard to match. You then pitch your offer slightly below the quoted price confirming your margin is very small. Once they hesitate on your inferior offer you then state "If I can match this extremely generous offer would you go ahead today?" You have now confirmed that 1) it was a good offer, 2) it is unlikely that shopping around will improve the price, and 3) closed it with a matching figure and personal charm.

CLOSE THE SALE

NO. 32

FEEL - FELT - FOUND CLOSE

When you are hit with an objection at the final closing stages it is good to have the above formula at your finger tips to conclude the sale.

Example

"Mary, I can understand how you feel about making a purchase while being six month's pregnant. A few times in the past women have told me they felt the same way. However, after being positive and going ahead they found that after the baby arrived they just would not have had the time to shop for this type of item."

When you work out and write down the above formula to suit your own product you will see how easy it is to use. Satisfying your buyer's needs and wants is what a selling career is all about so the sentences you construct and use are unique to you alone and are not being used by your competitors.

I use the formula occasionally in my seminars when a delegate might state that an idea I propose would not work at his showroom or place of work. My answer is always the same non-confrontational one.

Example

"John, I have had a number of salespeople such as yourself feel the way you did on hearing my suggestion. However when they felt they ought to give it a try 90% of them found it to be a great closing technique!"

CLOSE THE SALE

NO. 33

CASH BACK CLOSE

A cash back close can be used where the buyer is:

1) Buying on finance.

2) Has goods to trade-in.

One of the biggest markets over the last few years has been the re-mortgage market where people have been able to unlock the capital in their home when the property is worth much more than the outstanding mortgage.

If people have goods to trade-in such as trucks, boats, commercial vehicles, cars, motor-cycles, etc., this may be a very useful close for you to consider.

For instance, if the buyer is looking to purchase goods to the value of £10,000 and their offering is worth £3,600 you can attempt a close with cash back. Of course the amount of £3,600 needs to be fully paid and have no outstanding finance on it.

Most customers will not think about cash back in the negotiations unless you have an advertising campaign as such.

In the above example what you would say is similar to these words:

"Miss Calculation, my proposal is when you pick up your new van we will give you £1,600 cash to spend. With your own van covering 20% deposit your choice of payments would be:

4 years = £178.19 per month.

3 years = £239.14 per month.

2 years = £353.19 per month.

1 year = £668.19 per month.

Whichever you choose you will receive £1,600 of your money as cash back! Which would you prefer?"

N.B. You also make more profit on finance.

CLOSE THE SALE

NO. 34

MILLIONAIRE CLOSE

This television show is viewed in different formats throughout the world. I have already seen three different versions on my travels. For those who have not seen it I will explain.

By answering general knowledge questions the contestants can win up to one million Euro/pounds/dollars, etc. They are given the question with four possible answers from which they have to choose the correct one. If they do not know the answer they have three lifelines:

1) 50/50 - computer takes away two incorrect answers.

2) Ask the audience - they vote.

3) Phone a nominated friend.

Now, in a selling situation sometimes humour breaks the ice and during the last few years I have seen salespeople in quite different selling environments use what I now call the 'millionaire' close.

Example

"Mr. Field, we do not seem very far apart on price at the moment. May I ask you three questions:

1. Would you like to go 50/50?
2. Would you like to phone a friend?
3. Shall we ask the audience?"

I have seen much laughter, no anger and a good conversion rate of sales by introducing humour into a selected closing situation.

You may laugh all the way to the bank!

CLOSE THE SALE

NO. 35

BALANCE SHEET CLOSE

This particular close has been credited to Winston Churchill, the Duke of Wellington, Napoleon - prior to battle - and the wise old Benjamin Franklin. My own thoughts are that the latter deserves the credit. Millions of salespeople have been using this method for years. It is so simple to use, very basic and always manages to be received well by the buyer.

When the close originated it was meant to be used with notebook and pen. What you do is make a list with the help of the buyer showing all the positive things that they like about the proposed purchase. Having made a list of around 10-20 benefits agreed by the buyer, you now turn up the heat. Handing the piece of paper to the prospect and handing them your pen you ask them to write down any uncertainties they may have about the purchase. Of course during this time you give them no help whatsoever.

Whatever they write down are the objections they have to the sale. Probably outnumbered by 15-3 you point out that no purchase gives the buyer 100% concern free thoughts but 15 good reasons to buy must indicate how positive they are about going ahead.

Each of the three concerns must be treated as stumbling blocks on the way to the conclusion and have to be overcome to the buyer's satisfaction before asking for the order.

CLOSE THE SALE

IF YOU ARE A TOP CLOSER

DO NOT DISGUISE YOURSELF AS A LOSER!

NO. 36

HALF-NELSON CLOSE

This close has absolutely nothing to do with throwing your customer to the floor and putting his arm up his back. (Has there ever been any customer that you would like to have done that to?).

It is named the half-nelson close because the buyer has you in a difficult position. Mainly this occurs where the prospects indicate that they do not believe your words. To relieve yourself of this pressure it is always advisable to use documentary proof.

Example

"I do not believe that you only have a margin of £400 on that model."

Answer: "I must clarify the position to see if I have given you the right information. Let us both have a look at the manufacturer's wholesale price and compare it to our asking price."

Second Example

"I looked around here two months ago and that caravan was here then at a lower price than you are asking for now!"

Answer: "I might be mistaken so before we go any further let me check our records and show you the exact day the caravan arrived in our stock!"

With a half-nelson credibility statement always clarify with documentary proof!

CLOSE THE SALE

NO. 37

SIDE-STEP CLOSE

Great football, soccer, rugby players and boxers rely on a nifty side-step when facing opponents.

Sometimes you are sailing through your sales process and approaching the closing stages. Suddenly your buyer starts coming at you with relentless objections and this is where you need to side-step.

If you are sure that this product is the correct one for your customer then you need to try to avoid all objections being aimed at you.

Example

"Putting those points aside for one moment, Mr. Anderson, do you think you would like to enjoy the benefits our product offers?"

You see by side-stepping the situation, hopefully the buyer will realise he does want the advantages you have illustrated in your presentation. He will also realise that he is throwing too many concerns at you and avoiding his ultimate goal which is to buy.

Another Example

"Putting price aside for the moment, Mr. O'Reilly, would it be fair to say that this policy will benefit not only yourself but also your wife and two children?"

When people spend too much time throwing cost and price at you, a side-step is a good ploy to use.

CLOSE THE SALE

NO. 38

TOSS THE COIN CLOSE

I have no doubt that money is the greatest motivator of salespeople when they first join our industry. Why else would you have taken a job that keeps you working away from your friends and family for such long hours. Why then should we not from time to time use real money to close a sale. That is what the toss the coin close is.

To use this you must be negotiating with someone you know very well and have an under-standing of each other's sense of humour. People such as friends, family, previous clients spring to mind because this close is very assumptive.

When you are close to the sale and not very apart on price, you say to the buyer, "I have really gone as far as I can with regard to price but for a bit of fun I will toss you for another fifty pounds". At the same time as making this statement you take out of your pocket a one pound coin and toss it in the air. When you catch it you keep it covered and say to your buyer "heads or tails". You wait for the answer using the silent close. Provided they answer heads or tails they have bought. Why? Because when they call out their answer you glance at the coin out of sight of your buyer. If they have called correctly you show them and say "You win 50 pounds" but if they call the wrong number you put the coin back in your pocket and say exactly the same words "You win 50 pounds". It's a win-win situation; winners buy - losers walk.

CLOSE THE SALE

NO. 39

AUTOGRAPH CLOSE

I have mentioned rejection words during a previous close. For 30 years now I have said to salespeople sign is the worst of the lot. If you ask anybody to sign anything they are already thinking about how much fear they have encountered when asked to sign. Into their minds comes medical centres, solicitors, banks, government and all the things that caused them worry.

Once this warning signal has gone off they begin to hesitate in the negotiations. Never sign anything without a 48 hour 'thinking over' period is what they have been told.

My first sales manager taught me the autograph close.

I once saw him secure a sale worth around £150,000 of old age stock by turning the paperwork around and saying "I have been a fan of yours since we first met some three weeks ago. John, I would be delighted if I could have your autograph!" He handed the pen to the buyer who smiled and put pen to paper.

Now I believe in many, many closing situations salespeople would find that quite easy to do. I have used it selling vacuum cleaners door to door and Rolls Royce cars in Hong Kong.

Lighten up the situation. Rid yourself of rejection terminology and increase your sales results.

CLOSE THE SALE

NO. 40

COMMISSION CLOSE

A comment that used to annoy me as a salesperson was, "You are only interested in your commission". It has always been thought that salespeople would say anything just to earn a huge commission. Many people, especially those in non-sales employment, resented this fact.

You are selling to benefit the customer, not selling solely for the sake of selling. A sales-person who is professional, uses empathy and supplies goods for the benefit of other people, will continue on a successful selling career.

If you are a money grabbing self-motivated individual who will do and say anything, true or untrue just to gain your rewards, then you will not ultimately gain the job satisfaction we all crave.

If you are asked about your commission or receive a cynical remark questioning your motives (or even your parenthood), you need to explain the facts.

Example

"Our company, Mrs. Dobson, build into their price structure an amount of money for after-sales and customer care. My salary is part of that package and I am held responsible for every client I deal with to provide that service. I trust that clarifies the situation!"

By explaining the above you are not only doing yourself a favour, you also give your colleagues in our profession a better understanding from this type of buyer.

CLOSE THE SALE

ENTHUSIASM WILL LIFT YOU TO HIGHER EARNING LEVELS

NO. 41

REVERSAL CLOSE

This is the way to close "Mr. or Mrs. Non-committal". All through your presentation or sales pitch these people never show any buying signals, never nod their heads, avoid eye contact, and never say "Yes" to any of your "Say Yes" questions. What you have to achieve with this type of buyer is for them to say No at the closing stage to gain the sale.

Example No. 1

"In light of your previous comments that figure would not be a problem for you - would it?"

Ensure that you fully understand this process before embarking on it. When you make your offer or quote your price the buyer may mentally accept it but shows no outward signs of this to you. It may be that you can nudge them towards saying "Yes" but with this type of prospect it is difficult. Look for benefits that they may have glossed over - even minor ones. Always put yourself in their shoes (empathy) and try to understand what the buying motive is.

Never underestimate your client/buyer or the desire to purchase. Closing a satisfactory deal means that they think they have the best price and you know you have your best price.

Reversal Example No. 2

"This sofa is in stock and the right colour at a competitive price - you would not want to miss this opportunity, would you?"

CLOSE THE SALE

NO. 42

I'M JUST LOOKING CLOSE

Having worked in many showroom and display businesses during my selling career I realise the importance of the above statement.

I see so many salespeople in those situations say "How may I help you?" or similar, to which most people reply "I'm just looking". I find it incredible that so many staff then walk away from someone who is a buyer. We all say "I'm just looking" when we go shopping and are first approached, but it is a nervous reaction. Two minutes later we are looking for attention and then talk to a different salesperson. A lost sale for staff number one!

What we feel like saying in reply is:

> "I'm just looking" - "Hello, Mr. Looking or can I call you Just?"
>
> "I'm just looking" - "What do you think this is? A museum?"
>
> "I'm just looking" - "With or without your credit card?"
>
> "Can I look round" - "You look round enough to me, fatty."
>
> "I am just wasting time" - "You do look a waste of time but welcome."

Of course all the above we would not say because we are professionals - right?

To overcome this instant response mechanism we need to relax the buyers and commence conversation.

"I'm just looking" - "Are you looking to upgrade your present car?"

"I'm just looking" - "What type of ring are you considering?"

"I'm just looking" - "Can I show you our special offers?"

"I'm just looking" - "We have a number of machines I can show you."

"I'm just looking" - "What sort of dining suite would be ideal for your house?"

"I'm just looking" - "Let me bring over our latest brochure."

CLOSE THE SALE

NO. 43

STORE VOUCHER CLOSE

If you are selling any product that on average gives you in excess of £500 per unit then this close can increase your conversion rate by leaps and bounds. Caution is though that you will need management approval to use it.

Now your company may spend a small fortune on advertising to attract people to talk to you about your goods. What companies are not so thoughtful about is obtaining a second chance to talk to that person when the sale is lost.

When you part company with a buyer who says "I'll think about it", you sometimes feel like saying, "What are you going to use for equipment?" We do not say that though - do we?

In reality you have proposed an offer to your buyer who needs to give it more thought. The problem is two-fold. Firstly, your customer believes that is your best offer and, secondly, you cannot shout after them in the street, "Come back tomorrow and I will give you another £50 discount". The question is how many of those people would you sign up the next day if they came back and asked for £50 to finalise the transaction - plenty!

A simple company letter posted on the day of walk out to the buyer's address, signed by a manager, is what you need. Thank them for the visit, resell customer care, offer them a £50 store voucher in addition to any agreed figure if they give you an opportunity to reopen negotiations. Note - they have to buy to receive voucher!

CLOSE THE SALE

NO. 44

BRIDGING CLOSE

A great closer will be practising his skill all of the time. To some extent even in your personal life this desire to persuade people to your way of thinking becomes natural behaviour.

In the selling arena though you are faced with objections and obstacles which provide the challenges that we thrive upon.

Sometimes we are well into our presentation and have begun the closing questions and are hit with, "Tony, I do like your product and I know your company's reputation is first class, but I never make my mind up until I have had a few days looking at the pros and cons." To an average salesperson that is the end of the selling situation and he just hopes for a 'be-back'.

To a super salesperson though it is just a challenge to be met. This is where you need to build a bridge between your closes to allow a cooling off period of a few minutes before bringing the sale to a conclusion.

Example

"Mr. Copestack, I am sorry I was moving too quickly for you. I think my main reason for going so rapidly was that I could visualise you owning the caravan and enjoying your holidays." Now back off, talk sport, weather, family, kids, holidays, schools, etc. for around five/ten minutes. Introduce coffee/tea. Re-introduce closing statements into him after the break in proceedings.

CLOSE THE SALE

NO. 45

MANAGEMENT CLOSE

When you wander around a store or sales arena have you ever been approached by a salesperson whose face looks as if it has worn out three bodies. Have you ever been greeted by a frown and scowl and hurriedly been shown a product that you might be thinking of buying? On such occasions you look around for someone in authority who may be a lot more professional.

More often than not though the time when you would really like to talk to a manager is when it comes to price. If you were to say to a buyer, "Would you like me to give you our best price, madam, or would you like to talk to my manager about price?", what would they say? In 90% of cases they would want to talk to management. It has nothing to do with a manager being more professional it is solely to do with price! Everyone believes they will receive a better price the higher they go up the company ladder.

Now I am always surprised when salespeople believe they are losing credibility by involving management. By referring to a manager or head office for a final offer can increase your sales enormously.

If you cannot close the sale, introduce your supervisor, third party or manager into the arena. It will enhance your chance of a sale, not hinder it.

CLOSE THE SALE

YOU ARE NOT DEDUCTED MONEY IF YOU FAIL TO CLOSE BUT YOU ARE PAID MONEY WHEN YOU DO CLOSE!

ASK FOR THE BUSINESS!

NO. 46

CREDIT CARD CLOSE

For those of us in the profession of selling, the growth of the credit card industry has been a revolution. No more situations where we had to ask people to write out a cheque and authorise it. That was sometimes as hard for both parties than agreeing to the sale. Even asking for a small deposit in the days of the cheque could be a stumbling block to the sale.

Now we are in the world of plastic where, apart from cash, credit cards are the most welcome form of payment. It is instant and the buyers are so used to using them on a daily basis that very little fear lies in the use of them.

Credit cards have a number of uses when it comes to closing a sale.

Example

When a buyer is on the telephone enquiring about your goods you can immediately take a deposit or full payment. It has become sometimes easier to negotiate than in a face to face situation.

Example

Another example of a credit card close is where you are face to face in negotiation. You may be £300 apart on price but then you turn round and say "Mr. Terry, we have facilities here for MasterCard, Visa, etc., why don't you put the £300 differential onto your card and you can then settle that when it is more convenient!"

CLOSE THE SALE

NO. 47

NO DEPOSIT CLOSE

Have you ever been in a situation where you achieve a close but the buyer states that they cannot leave a deposit. The reason can be that whilst they are happy to agree the contract they have left their wallet in the car, or at home or do not carry a cheque book with them.

Your company policy may or may not be that a deposit has to be taken.

The biggest thing we are concerned about here though is commitment. A buyer who has not paid a deposit will not feel as locked into the deal as someone who has. It rarely happens these days that people go out to purchase without financial ability. Sometimes however it is used as an excuse so they do not pay the deposit and lose nothing financially if they cancel within a couple of days.

When this situation arises one way to overcome the problem is this. State that your company will not accept orders without deposit but under the circumstances you personally will pay the amount into the company accounts office. Ask them then to forward a cheque or phone in credit card details during the next 72 hours. You would then hold the order form until their deposit was forthcoming without processing the sale.

The advantage of this 'no deposit close' is that the buyer feels even more committed believing you have paid his deposit personally.

CLOSE THE SALE

NO. 48

DEMONSTRATION CLOSE

Selling is not a spectator sport. Your buyers need to be involved in the whole process not just the closing arena.

Should you be selling computers to competent operators do not use the machine yourself. Let them perform the functions so that they feel involved in the whole process. People will not buy clothes, shoes, engagement rings, etc. without trying them on so this should also be the same with larger products. I have seen so many salespeople baffle people with product knowledge while showing a washing machine or cooker. Stepping back and letting them press a few buttons and ask a few questions sometimes brings a better conclusion.

A truck salesperson told me last year that he always requests to take out the probable driver of the truck after his presentation to the company buyer. When out with the driver he pulls over and changes places. After making sure he is comfortable with all the controls he says, "Okay, away you go - pretend it's yours". Should the driver be impressed with the truck you know you will have him on your side when the boss says to him, "What do you think!" That is a demonstration close.

A touch it - feel it - drive it demonstration gives the potential buyer the opportunity to see that what the salesperson has been saying in theory, does in fact work in practice.

CLOSE THE SALE

NO. 49

CONSENT CLOSE

Making a proposal is the basic principle of all negotiations. You have to decide at the right moment whether you are going to give your figure first, or you are going to respond to their offer. Your decision will be a crucial part of the closing stage.

Try to present your first figure with as little emotion as possible and leave yourself plenty of room to negotiate.

Remember that debating the close is as much about listening as it is about talking. You should be clear about your objectives and do not present your final offer until the atmosphere is cordial. It is no good presenting a 'final offer' of £7,500 to which they say "It is unacceptable" and then going in at a better price of £7,000. You can lose your credibility big time with that one.

A consent close is where you are met with total silence when you present your offer. To break the ice and hopefully close the sale you announce, "My first manager, who was a very experienced businessman, always instilled in me, Mrs. Lopez, that silence meant consent. Because you have not rejected our offer can I ascertain that I have covered every single point to your satisfaction?

Consenting to the offer means that we can take the piano off sale and busy ourselves arranging delivery. Tuesday or Thursday are our delivery days, which would you prefer?"

CLOSE THE SALE

NO. 50

CONSTANT QUESTIONS CLOSE

Recently I was conducting a seminar in the north of England. One salesperson described his manager as "An answer looking for the right question"! He meant that his boss never asked questions but always knew the answers. Now that may be okay in a management position but not for the professional salesperson in conversation with a buyer. Questions are the way to close.

Watch David Frost interview people, watch QCs and attorneys on television interviewing witnesses. Their job, like yours and mine, depends on asking the right questions, doesn't it?

If a child wants a hamster she should start by asking for a pony. If a boy wants a pair of top football boots he should ask his parents how he should spend his money when he is as famous as David Beckham.

A number of small questions can lead to the final big agreement. Use your questions to confirm statements and make final requests.

Say someone tells you that economy is very important to them in buying a new car. When you are ready to ask them for a final decision go ahead like this: "Didn't you say that fuel economy was your primary concern?" This starts the yes momentum and you just keep adding those tie-down questions to lead them to the sale.

Selling requires many agreements before the buyer puts pen to paper. If they are not agreeing to your questions you are not in control. Good questions get your prospect thinking in the affirmative.

CLOSE THE SALE

YOU WILL NEVER FIND A GREAT CLOSER LACKING IN QUESTIONS!

NO. 51

INDECISION CLOSE

This closing technique is to be used when you know they want your product but are being evasive in giving you the go ahead answer.

In this situation it is important to reiterate your benefits and do so slowly and methodically. Try to present the advantages of purchase with a new and fresh approach. Clarify your priorities and be ready to concede on less important issues.

When a deal looks near to conclusion there is often sensitivity on both sides. What amount of time is spent after reaching a verbal agreement and the contract/order being signed is very delicate. Some salespeople lose the sale between these two points. If the customer is hesitant, sympathise with them. Explain how important the deal is to you also, that you would value their making a positive decision.

Show that you are a good listener by nodding your head and looking at them eye to eye. It is not what they say that counts but the meaning behind the words. Never argue with the customer, i.e. win the argument - lose the sale situation.

Point out how many times in your life you have lost obvious benefits through indecision.

For example:

A) An apartment you wanted to rent.

B) A house you wanted to purchase.

C) A holiday with friends.

D) A piece of furniture in a sale.

By pointing out your disappointment through lack of decisiveness can sway your buyer to have a fear of loss if they do not buy.

CLOSE THE SALE

NO. 52

BENEFITS RECAP CLOSE

Most people like to own the very best of things for their family and themselves. Nobody likes to admit that what they purchased in the past was the wrong decision. Try to get the buyer's mind on to owning your product and off the possible price objection.

Remember that negotiating involves two or more persons who each have something the other wants, reaching agreement through a process of bargaining.

Remind your buyer or client that the only time they really benefited from anything in life was when they said yes not no!

They might have said yes when they joined a local football team and yes when they selected a school or college. Most likely they said yes when they chose their partner and yes to the property they now live in.

No doubt they said yes when they took their current job and yes when they bought their current car.

I am sure they said yes to all the clothes they are now wearing.

Example

"All the things that you enjoy in life you said yes to! I assure you that if you say yes to this product you will feel just the same! Don't you agree?"

CLOSE THE SALE

NO. 53

SECONDARY QUESTION CLOSE

A secondary question close is an alternative close put onto the end of a proposal.

Example

"I've had a word with my supervisor and we can offer you the table at £814.19. Would you like to take delivery this week or next week?"

After presenting your price you just carry on talking, building in the alternative questions at the end of your statement.

Think of every close that I mention in this book as another piece towards your completed jigsaw. If you have some weaknesses in your sales process you need to review and learn as quickly as possible.

As you become a more successful salesperson you will find these new skills will become natural to you. Between your progress and perfection there will be a gap, so give your colleagues, management and most important clients time to adjust to the new you.

Another example

"I've worked out the figures on this office desk to £432.19 which I am sure you will agree is fair and reasonable, but may I ask you - do you need the chair you looked at to go with it?"

You see whatever the answer is regarding the chair they will still have bought the desk as long as they answer the alternative will you - won't you close regarding the chair.

CLOSE THE SALE

NO. 54

QUALIFICATION CLOSE

There is a well known saying, "If you think training is expensive consider the cost of ignorance". The chances of your company sending you on a seminar where you would study so many tips on closing are remote. By obtaining this book you have taken a great leap in self-improvement and should climb to the top of the sales ladder very rapidly.

A qualification close is to be used when you are working with a product where medical or credit rating checks are necessary.

Because of the type of product it is, many buyers will not feel any urgency to conclude the agreement. This can be frustrating as you go for the close. What you do with the qualification close is infer that they may not qualify so it would be a good idea to check that immediately.

Example

"Mr. Spencer, I would like to talk to you about how 90% of our clients fund their super-market displays. Shall we see if this is an option you would like to take?"

By filling in a credit application form you can go for the close.

Example

"Mr. Conway, with your irregular heartbeat it may be that an insurance company would need to set you up with a thorough medical before acceptance. I think we should take details down subject to approval."

CLOSE THE SALE

NO. 55

MARKET EDGE CLOSE

You may be selling to companies who are in a very competitive market.

When discussing terms with your clients or potential clients it is always advisable to hint that you are fully aware that they are in a market place that has lots of competition. They need to be reminded at this time that they, like you, need to survive in this business world of ours.

Reiterate the fact that the competitors that they do have are faced with the same day to day problems as them. Confirm the fact that you are informed with the knowledge that, whilst all companies have the same challenges to meet, some deal with them better than others!

You need to explain that the purpose of your visit and keeping in regular touch with them is to make sure they have the market edge. Your product will save them money, enhance their national and local profit and give satisfaction to their staff.

It is a good idea to go armed with documentary evidence of your statements in case you need to produce material to support your proposals and claims.

You are there to help them make a decision they, in most cases, have already decided on. They would not waste time talking to you about your product if they did not want to buy it.

CLOSE THE SALE

POSITIVE THINKING CLOSES
NEGATIVE THINKING FAILS!

NO. 56

MOTIVE CLOSE

Before you go for the close it is important to establish the buying motive of the buyer. If the customer is very slow in communicating, it is necessary to ask the right questions to gain the right information. Your prospect may appear to have had a charisma by-pass operation but they still know why they want to purchase. Remember that 80% of people are "I want" buyers and only 20% "I need" buyers.

In my opinion the dictionary is the only place where success comes before training. I have always told sales teams to remember the word CARPASS.

C	=	COST
A	=	APPEARANCE
R	=	RELIABILITY
P	=	PERFORMANCE
A	=	AMBITION
S	=	SAFETY
S	=	SEX APPEAL

It is most likely that your buyer will be mainly concerned with one or two of the above and that is what you have to find out. Be assertive but not aggressive when closing a deal. Find out what the "hot buttons" are and press not once but as many times as it takes. Failure to qualify the motivation behind the enquiry can end in failure.

CLOSE THE SALE

NO. 57

SECOND BEST CLOSE

When you are faced with a situation where your customers indicate that they are shopping around on price this is the one to use.

One of the largest retail groups in the United Kingdom advertise the following slogan at all their outlets and in any TV or newspaper marketing: "If after your purchase you find the same product at a cheaper price, we will refund the difference". From a turnover of billions how many customers take up the challenge after purchase? Less than 1% I am informed. 99% of people just assume it is a very competitive price. Of course it also saves the company hundreds of thousands of pounds in market research trying to be the very lowest price in the market place.

When you are negotiating you must explain fully the terms of you agreement. Use your knowledge and training to help you present your 'first price'. The terms of your proposal may involve method of payment, timescale of payment, guarantee, extended warranty and any accessory packages you may want to sell.

When faced with this buyer who indicates he is price orientated say something along these lines:

Example

"We have our product here ready for immediate/imminent delivery and I would state it is firm company policy to be first not only in customer care but also in competitive pricing of our goods!"

CLOSE THE SALE

NO. 58

PERSONAL REWARD CLOSE

This close is used to show buyers that they really deserve what they are about to purchase. Most people feel they have achieved something in their life when they make a purchase. Non-achievers would probably not have the money to spend anyway. People do not wander through life feeling they are not worthy of some reward from time to time.

Buyers have a basic need, probably since childhood, for recognition by others. I will quote you an example of a personal reward close which happened to me a few years ago.

I was working with one of my clients in a showroom management role and one of the sales team was trying to convince a married couple in their forties to purchase a particular product. He was unable to close so introduced me into the arena. Whilst sitting talking to the couple the lady, who was the main decision maker, told me she was in the teaching profession and had just been made a head teacher. I asked her how long she had been in the profession and she said 20 years. I then made the following closing statement: "You have been in your profession for 20 years and it must always have been your ambition to be a head teacher eventually. Many congratulations on achieving your goal. You obviously like our product. You only need to answer me one question - when is the best time to reward yourself with something you know you can afford?"

Of course the answer was "now!"

CLOSE THE SALE

NO. 59

EMPATHY CLOSE

Do not ever confuse sympathy with empathy. Sympathy costs you profit, empathy does not.

Empathy is about putting yourself in other people's shoes and trying to understand how they think and feel. For over 20 years of carrying out seminars and training courses I always try to be empathetic to my students. My friends and family often ask me if I have rude or disruptive people at my work. In all honesty I can say that not once has the situation ever occurred. By nature I am not a confrontational person and if you try to understand how the other person feels you will succeed in selling and in life.

Ask yourself next time you are selling: "What will this product do for them, will they find it efficient? Will it be cost saving and value for money for them? Can they afford it? What do they think of me as a person?" By asking yourself these questions you are putting yourself in their shoes.

If you know what they are thinking and how they feel about you and your product you will know when to ask the question!

Will they look better, sleep better, feel better with your product?

We have all seen men at parties chatting up ladies who have no interest in them whatsoever. If we can see it - why can't they? Because they have no empathy (or are inebriated).

Once you have climbed inside your buyer's head, asking for their business is easy.

CLOSE THE SALE

NO. 60

NEGOTIATION CLOSE

Let us look at an example of the negotiation close.

You have reached the stage where you are about to present your proposal and you pitch at an investment of £10,000. You know at a push you could accept £9,500.

On receiving your figure of £10,000 the buyer indicates that his offer is £9,000 which he is prepared to pay now! So you are £1,000 apart with £500 to play with.

I see so many salespeople in this situation who, because they are so far apart on price, go straight back in at £9,500, mumbling something about meeting them halfway. The problem is the buyer is not convinced that this was their 'best price' and the salesperson had no more money left on the table.

What you should do in that situation is go back with an offer of £9,800 and try to close. If this does not work you should ask the buyer to help you by increasing his offer by a similar amount, i.e. £9,200. Now you are only £600 apart.

Your next offer should be a further £200 reduction to £9,600 and a trial close. If you fail you should then ask the buyer to help you by a similar amount, i.e. £9,400. Now only £200 apart!

When you then try the 50/50 meet you in the middle close both of you are happy. The buyer feels he squeezed an extra £500 out of you and you, by increases of £200 Ü £200 Ü £100, reached your final price.

CLOSE THE SALE

IF YOU STAND STILL IN LEARNING YOU GET OVERTAKEN VERY QUICKLY!

NO. 61

'I'LL THINK ABOUT IT' CLOSE

When your buyer says these magical words to you what do you feel like saying. "What a pity, I thought we were going to have a battle of wits, but I see you have come unarmed". We may feel like saying that, but we don't and never will, will we?

If a situation arises and you have greeted your buyer, qualified their needs and carried out a thoroughly polished presentation of your product, it is time to close.

The problem arises that although you know they want to go ahead on emotion that little thing called logic gets in the way and stalemate occurs.

Example

When people used to say to me "I'll think about it", I would just sit back relaxed in my chair using my own body language to take off the pressure. I would then say to them, "So that I can give the matter some more thought while you go away to think about it, could you please give me some indication of what you need to think over! Is it me? Is it the product? Is it the company? Is it the delivery date?"

Once I had highlighted why buyer's remorse had set in I suggested they had a cup of coffee, spent time alone in my office and came to a decision.

It is wise at this point, if appropriate, to mention that this product is in short supply and with a national sales force may not be available tomorrow!

CLOSE THE SALE

NO. 62

BOX OF CHOCS CLOSE

Whether on a diet or not how do most people feel when they eat one of those glorious Ferrero Rocher chocolates that are prettily gift wrapped in a box of eight? Most people love them and only feel good things while digesting.

A good idea in certain selling situations is to stock a few boxes of these, readily available for "I'll think about it" closing situation. Taste is one of the six senses and smell is another which is another benefit of chocolate.

When your buyer cannot be closed for genuine reasons and needs to go away and think things over then up comes the box of chocs close!

"Thank you for visiting us today, Mrs. Coates, and I am sure you will find this carpet will enhance the comfort in your very tastefully furnished home. While you are thinking things over with your husband tonight please accept this small gift for your initial interest - I hope you enjoy them!"

How many times have I had people come back and say, "I will buy if I can have another box of chocolates", said with a beaming smile on their face.

If it is a man you are negotiating with, sometimes it is appropriate to give a box of chocolates for him and his partner to enjoy while mulling things over.

CLOSE THE SALE

NO. 63

TOP DRAWER CLOSE

Some 20 years ago I learned an excellent close from a general manager in London called Jack Thrower. Now Jack used to listen into my 'Close that Sale' seminars with great enthusiasm. Although Jack was ten years older than me he was always hungry for knowledge.

I will explain Jack's top drawer close shortly. Closing is about negotiating which affects us all in daily life. You may agree to take your son to football training with his friends once a month, but you make sure the other parents are on the rota. I have to negotiate with my wife each time we go to the cinema, have a meal out or go on holiday. When you put your house up for sale and enter the housing market, prices go up and down more times than a lavatory seat at a mixed party.

So everything we do is negotiable so we need to learn how to close.

The top drawer close shown to me by Jack so many years ago I have taught many people to use and have in fact used it in private negotiations myself.

When a customer came to Jack Thrower's office and he had made them a proposal which was rejected, he never gave a final offer. If the buyer then said he was going to shop around on price this is what happened. Jack simply wrote down on a piece of paper a price hidden from the customer. He put it in an envelope with the customer's name on it and said, "My final offer I will put in the top drawer. Let us compare your other quotes, I am very confident." It always brought people back!

CLOSE THE SALE

NO. 64

TRIAL CLOSE

A trial close is used to commit the buyer to the purchase by talking about accessories, add-ons or finance, etc.

Example

"The suit really looks good on you, Mr. Phillips, would you like a matching tie?"

If Mr. Phillips agrees to the tie then you know he has bought your suit.

Example

"I am sure that this machine will make a huge difference to your home, Miss Issipi. You will be taking advantage of the two year warranty with credit protection, won't you?"

By agreeing to the warranty Miss Issipi will have bought the machine.

Example

"As you can see, Robert, this car has really been kept in first class condition and is within your budget. Will you be paying cash or using our finance?"

In answering the question regarding finance he is buying the car.

Do not read this book once and forget the closes. Set yourself a target of adapting them to suit your business. Then work out how many you can master per month and eventually they will become second nature.

Example

"After you have read this book you will try some of these closes, won't you?"

NB - Hopefully I am committing you by trial close to read the book.

CLOSE THE SALE

NO. 65

YES CLOSE

In 99% of selling situations we are using all our personal, presentation and closing skills trying to attract the all important Yes from the buyer.

Well, the big yes is arrived at by all the minor yes's you have gained along the way by your questioning skill. I always teach salespeople to start the "Yes" game as soon as you meet people. It is great fun as you tick them off in your head waiting to go for the big one! It is so much easier to close someone if they have said yes to five or six of your questions prior to the ultimate finish. Try not to use them consecutively!

Examples of gaining "yes's" to lead you to the sale are as follows:

1. "Good morning, a beautiful day today, isn't it?"
2. "After 12 years it really is time you upgraded your cooker, don't you think?"
3. "A critical illness policy would put your mind at rest over the mortgage repayments, wouldn't it?"
4. "You really have looked after your present car, haven't you?"
5. "Your wife will make her friends envious with that coat on, won't she?"
6. "Upgrading your computer systems will also have a motivational effect on your staff, won't it?"
7. "Our asking price is fair and reasonable, isn't it?"

CLOSE THE SALE

NO ASK - NO CLOSE!

NO. 66

DELIVERY CLOSE

A delivery close can be used when the goods you are selling have to be prepared for delivery or delivered to the buyer's premises or home.

Let me assume that you have excellent selling skills, and can converse comfortably with any type of buyer you meet. You have most likely spent many years practising your skills. They say that a picture paints a thousand words so you are out there with paint brush and canvas illuminating your buyer's darkness.

You know that the product you are selling is the latest model and it has obvious advantages over its predecessor and competition models. You also know all its functions and what the colour range is. Also you know how much the cost is and what special rates your finance department will authorise.

You now ask your buyer for his business and he says, "I will let you know in three or four days' time".

To use the delivery close you say something similar to this. "Mr. Lee, you mentioned that having delivery by the end of the month is important to you. As a company we have one large preparation and delivery depot. The problem is though with a national sales force 245 strong we could take orders for over a thousand units in the next few days. It would mean that we could not start preparation or deliver your product until the others are dealt with. A decision now would put you at the front of the queue and guarantee delivery!"

CLOSE THE SALE

NO. 67

LET'S PRETEND IT'S TOMORROW CLOSE

I am often asked if I consider closing methods are in the best interests of my clients. I have said many times before that people know what they want and just need a salesperson to lead them to a conclusion.

My selling career has taken me to four continents to work and I always have been honest in my delivery to my buyers. Having a vast knowledge of closing tips, methods and techniques has given me various processes to follow with different types of selling situations.

I have worked with salespeople who have been dishonest in their approach and those people either ended up in prison or fired by a succession of selling organisations.

Now, a let's pretend it's tomorrow close is fun to use. If you are sitting with a customer at the negotiation stage they often say the words, "I'll let you know tomorrow". One of my answers was this: "Mr. Paxton, thank you for listening to my presentation and our company's proposal. Let me ask you this, let's pretend it's tomorrow. When you do contact me, what is it that you will be telling me? Will it be positive or negative? Have I explained everything I should have to you or is it the price we will discuss? To save time, we should deal with tomorrow today!"

CLOSE THE SALE

NO. 68

END USER CLOSE

Your customers say to themselves:

- I am spending money so I want to be treated with respect.
- Qualify me correctly, treat me as an individual.
- Show me how your product will benefit me.
- Explain the facts so I can make a decision.
- What problems will you solve for me.
- How will we do business? How will it be delivered? Who will I deal with? What about repairs and after-sales service?

Because you have to satisfy all the above you realise that a closing question has to be very special. When a closing question is answered it should tell you that the buyer has reached the maximum point of interest and wants to go ahead. When you ask a closing question you are looking for the answer that will give you the order.

You need to be professional at the closing stage and my opinion is that a professional knows his job inside out. I do bear in mind though that amateurs built the Ark and professionals built the Titanic, so do not be over-confident at the point of sale or it will be a sink or swim situation for you also.

An end user close example is as follows.

Salesperson: "Tell me, will you be the people utilising this lawn mower or will someone else be the user?"

When they tell you who is going to use the mower they have bought it, haven't they?

CLOSE THE SALE

NO. 69

PUPPY DOG CLOSE

It is surprising in my seminars how many people have not heard of the 'puppy dog' close. Many years ago it was one of the first tips given to me as I started my selling career.

Where did it obtain its name? In the United States when someone visited a pet shop and saw a beautiful little puppy the shop owner said, "Take the little fella home for seven days at no cost and if you don't like him bring him back!" What happened? Within hours the puppy was loved by the whole family and in spite of unnecessary deposits on the carpet there would be no taking young Fido back to the shop.

One of the first industries to adopt this method of selling in the 1950s were TV shops. 14 days' free trial of a new TV set in your lounge meant it never went back.

Today timeshare and holiday home companies are forever offering "free weekends" for you to look over the golf course and wonderful facilities. All you have to do is attend a one hour sales presentation.

Motor manufacturers and dealers use it, airline companies tempt you, local hotels offer free nights, etc. It is all geared for you to obtain temporary ownership. Even my company do one hour free presentations - why?

If it suits your business - puppy dog them.

<u>CLOSE THE SALE</u>

NO. 70

FINANCE CLOSE

In many selling situations you are also selling your product on finance. Also it may be that they are trading in a product that is on finance.

If you suspect or know this is the case with the part-exchange always avoid asking the question "Have you any outstanding finance?" or, worse still, "How much do you owe on your present boat/house/car, etc." It is much less confrontational to ask "Have you a settle-ment figure that we can build into the negotiations?" It sounds more professional and does not embarrass the buyer.

How many salespeople do I hear saying to potential buyers the words, "What is your budget?", or "How much do you want to spend?", or, worse still, "What can you afford or go up to?" Imagine going to dinner with your partner and after asking for a table for two the maître d' asks you the above questions. Would you be impressed? I think not! You are leaning on an open door unless you introduce finance payments in the correct manner.

Verbally, always ask what weekly figure they have in mind - not monthly.

Remember £200 per month is £200.

£50 per week is £216 per month.

Having asked what weekly figure they have in mind always say "and up to".

N.B. £55 per week is £236 per month!

CLOSE THE SALE

A SATISFACTORY CLOSE NEEDS A SATISFACTORY BEGINNING!

NO. 71

"WHAT IS YOUR BEST PRICE?" CLOSE

When I worked in the Middle and Far East in sales I had to get used to the culture. One of the things I noticed was that everyone asked for 'the best price'! Now if you are in a senior management role it is very simple to deal with. The problem was that my sales force were young men and women (Far East only - NB - Middle East women do not work) who were put under immense pressure in showrooms when asked that question. An additional factor in the East was that staff did not want to lose face in front of their clients.

What I have always told my staff, and latterly students, is that when you are approached in this manner you need to slow the proceedings down. It is no good giving a figure which they will immediately shop somewhere else.

My instructions were to say "The best price I can get for you is one my manager will approve. Let us sit down and work a proposal out". Now this method immediately took the pressure off the salesperson and slowed down the whole process.

Of course a certain type of buyer would turn round and say, "Let me talk to your manager, then!"

My office door was always open (until they had entered the room) and then I would go through my 'never let the sun go down on a good offer' theory.

CLOSE THE SALE

NO. 72

SELL WHAT THEY WANT CLOSE

Many salespeople only sell what they like selling and generally only to people that they like. Of course it is helpful to sell a product that you believe in but not always possible to be selling the market leader. As I said before though, and I repeat, "You do not have to like people you sell to but get everyone to like you!" Keep your mind open.

Do not prejudge people as soon as you see them. Do not judge people on appearance, physical condition, clothing, hairstyle or walk.

An example of anything to everybody close from my own experience illustrates why salespeople need to take their customers as they find them.

On a Saturday early in my sales career, a couple pulled up outside the company I was working at. They drove a beat-up van and their clothes suggested they worked on a pig farm Another salesperson in our showroom took one look at them and said, "Tony, you can deal with Mr. and Mrs. Farmer, good luck!" He walked away leaving me to talk to the unkempt couple.

As it turned out they were looking for two new cars. They were in the farming business and owned a sizeable house with farmland out of town. I helped them find their new vehicles. A few months later they came back to me to buy a new van. Over the years, I sold them more vehicles and to top it all made handsome profits on the part-exchanges. Had I prejudged those people by appearance, I may have been the one to walk away from some large commissions.

Don't let appearances fool you and sell your product. Always act as if each buyer is an important part of your life.

CLOSE THE SALE

NO. 73

TIME LIMIT CLOSE

One thing I learned as a young recruit from a salesperson was that people would suddenly look at their watch and say something like "Oh, is that the time? I must go and pick up the kids - I will ring you tomorrow". In many cases I never saw them again as it was just their excuse to break off a closing situation.

After seeking advice I was soon able to remedy that type of problem.

If someone walked into a selling situation very early in my qualification I would say "How much time have you got available for me to show you this product and all its benefits?" If the answer was "I've only called in for some quick information and a price because I have a meeting in half an hour in town", I would simply reappoint when they had more time rather than try to close. If the answer was "Oh, I'm okay for time - it is my day off", it was a green light to go for the order.

Even today when I go to someone's office for a 3.00 pm appointment I will immediately ask "How long have we got before your next appointment?" If the answer is "My next meeting is at 4.00 pm" I will reply, "So as long as I am out of here by 3.45 pm you are happy". Once confirmed, I have now got 45 minutes to close him down.

Once you have your buyer committed to a time span you know they cannot easily walk out and you know how long you have to sell.

<u>CLOSE THE SALE</u>

NO. 74

ORDER FORM CLOSE

My wife and I have purchased many different type of goods over the years from properties to television sets. On many, many occasions I have had the order form close worked on me and in most cases without objection.

An order form close is when you simply write all the details of the sale onto an order form and ask the buyer to sign it. Easy, isn't it?

If you have sold yourself (your first step), qualified the buyer, presented your product, talked of the benefits your company offers and demonstrated the goods, it should be no problem. This is provided you have read the situation correctly and seen the buying signals.

Dealing is 90% selling and 10% closing. Now if you try 10% selling you are left with 90% closing. This will certainly not work in most instances with the order form close.

Many buyers will respond favourably after a good presentation if you say, "Now we have found a suitable product for you to consider, let us put some details on paper to see how it works out. If you are happy you can okay the paperwork and if not we will put it in the waste bin". In some selling situations paperwork is not necessary apart from the receipt (lucky you!), but if essential, try the above method.

CLOSE THE SALE

NO. 75

PLEA CLOSE

To be introduced in a situation where you have put a lot of time and effort into presenting your product. You need to highlight your disappointment if they do not go ahead. Emphasise the agreements you have regarding the negotiations. Always be polite and friendly as this will gain you respect.

Around 20% of sales are made on logic and 80% on emotion. Pleading to a buyer's emotions makes them feel guilty if they do not purchase the product. Note that this tactic can sometimes work against you so select the type of person you work it on. People who feel they have been emotionally manipulated may be even more unwilling to agree a deal.

If you negotiate through a third party or manager you can use this skill quite effectively.

I do not agree with salespeople telling people they are overdrawn at the bank, about to lose their house or job or even worse they have a family of six to feed. Sitting down with a face like a bulldog chewing a wasp and weeping does not fool anyone.

Try these examples:

1. "Is it something I have not explained to you properly?"
2. "Was something wrong in my presentation?"
3. "I've just told my manager you really wanted it!"
4. "Is it a personality problem?"
5. "I have really enjoyed our two hour discussions - have you?"

CLOSE THE SALE

THERE ARE NO SECOND PRIZES IN CLOSING!

NO. 76

HOT POTATO CLOSE

This technique has been effective for many years and can be used in many selling situations.

If I was holding a piping hot baked potato and threw it at you, what would happen? You might say you would eat it but in most cases you would throw it straight back at me.

Sometimes a buyer will throw a statement at you so that they can leave the premises and "think about it". As it is your job to close the sale you have to respond with skill. They have thrown the 'hot potato' - don't duck or eat it - throw it back!

Examples

1. Customer: "I don't know whether the car will fit in my garage!"

   Salesperson: "Let us take the car to your house and try. It is an important factor!"

2. Customer: "I am not sure my husband wants to spend so much on this watch for my birthday."

   Salesperson: "As he has left the choice to you, please use our telephone and contact him in private to see if you can go ahead!"

3. Customer: "We are not sure how this Persian rug would look in our lounge."

   Salesperson: "You must then lay it down on your floor to see. I will bring all three you have looked at to your house to compare! Would 6.00 pm tonight or 10.00 am tomorrow be more suitable?"

CLOSE THE SALE

NO. 77

INFERIOR PRODUCT CLOSE

Every buyer is looking at value for money but when using hard earned cash do not want an inferior product.

This close can be used with a person who likes your product but is trying to persuade you to accept a lower price.

You must study and rehearse negotiating to improve your conversion rate. Closing is a skill most people can learn and there are plenty of opportunities to study. Basic things you have to learn for successful negotiations include your products, company history and an ability to understand objectives. You also want to be flexible and have the ability to explore and explain each possible option. You must have the self discipline to prepare well, listen and have interactive competence. Being able to prioritise is also a necessity.

Examples of inferior product close:

1. "While I cannot accept your offer and reduce this vehicle by £300, I have some new information. We have a car, same year, but in green, 11,000 more miles, not so nice regarding bodywork and has two more owners - that would be available at the price you suggest - would you be interested?"
2. "Your offer on the house has not been accepted but I may be able to show you another property."
3. "At that price I could only run the policy for 15 years not 20 as you wished!"

N.B. To use this close you must know they are sold on the product.

CLOSE THE SALE

NO. 78

UPGRADE CLOSE

When concluding a sale and making a proposal I do not like to hear salespeople talking about 'price to change' or 'cost to change' or, likewise, 'the price will be' or 'the cost will be'. Both the words cost and price are rejection words in the selling world. Nobody likes to pay a price and nobody relishes cost. Upgrade is something everyone wants. You can have an upgrade at McDonalds, in hotels, on aeroplanes and theatre bookings, etc. So bear in mind that when you offer your buyer a product they want to be 'upgrading' their lifestyle.

Why does a top salesperson make selling look so natural. Hours, days and even years have gone into the planning and preparation for just a few minutes face-to-face negotiation. If you think you have to know every skill in selling you will fail. I am still learning today even though I pass on my thoughts and process to thousands of eager sales teams. Remember we are all experts on limited knowledge. If you agree that there is always a need to improve your skills you are on the right track. The day you have no need to increase your knowledge is possibly the day you will die.

Example upgrade close

"Miss Conduct, I have worked out that the figure for you to upgrade your washing machine will be £396.14."

CLOSE THE SALE

NO. 79

'LOST MEMORY' CLOSE

You may have to negotiate many times with people who will compare your retail selling price with your competitors. Before I explain the 'lost memory' close I want you to consider:

Why do people not buy from a sales person?

A) Cost.

B) Reputation.

C) Warranty.

D) Salesperson.

E) Location.

F) Product.

In any survey our company carries out the number one reason why people buy a particular article is No. D (salesperson). Also, the number one reason why people do not buy is also D) (salesperson).

This shows that people are not always what they seem; 'shopping around for the best price'. A 'lost memory' close is when you say in total sincerity, "I cannot remember the last time I lost a sale on price!" You can say this because you know if any buyer was that impressed with your professional manner they would have bought irrespective of price. As I have said before, most people are not shopping around for the best price only one that is fair and reasonable. Nobody gets 'the best' price unless you are selling well below cost price.

Promise me you are not!

CLOSE THE SALE

NO. 80

MULTIPLE PAYMENT CLOSE

In many sales operations you have to sell your goods on finance. A multiple choice payment close is much more acceptable to your buyer than a 'take it or leave it' attempt to conclude the deal.

It is important that you present your proposal with a confident manner and give firm indications that you have studied the options. Before laying down the figures, emphasise the need to reach an agreement due to a well thought out fear factor. When making your proposal be clear what the figures include and what is not covered. Repeat the figures and show that you have finished by allowing your buyer to digest your words.

I am always annoyed to see the 'take it or leave it' proposal.

Example

Buyer - "Could you tell me how much it will cost over two years?"

Salesperson (after calculation) - £214.33 per month!"

Winners buy - losers walk. This buyer will not feel comfortable in accepting because they need choice!

A better answer would be: "1 year = £428.66.

2 years = £214.33.

3 years = £142.33.

4 years = £107.16.

Which are you happier to choose?"

N.B. Always show at least four choices when presenting financial terms and state whether or not it includes payment protection.

CLOSE THE SALE

IF YOU LEARN WHEN TO CLOSE YOUR MOUTH

YOU CAN CLOSE THE SALE!

NO. 81

"THANK YOU FOR YOUR OFFER" CLOSE

This close should be used when the buyer makes you an offer that you cannot accept.

Example No. 1

"Thank you very much for your offer which I accept is a large sum to invest. However on this particular model it is not enough - shall we look at something in a different price range?"

If they cannot afford to pay any more they may opt to look at a less expensive item. However if they are totally sold on the original item they usually say "What is your lowest price?" In most cases you can then negotiate to a conclusion.

Successful closing is an attempt by two or three people to achieve a mutually acceptable figure. It should not result in one winner and one loser.

This process should end with a satisfactory conclusion for both sides. Negotiation is an art where you need to recognise the buyer's 'wants and needs'. To achieve this goal where both parties win something for themselves you need to be well prepared, alert and empathetic.

Example No. 2

"Thank you for your offer but on this model we have not the facility to move that far on the margin. Please could you reconsider your offer under these circumstances." - Silence!

CLOSE THE SALE

NO. 82

HOT COFFEE CLOSE

When I started my selling career I was employed and managed by a huge Irish sales director. On my first day at work he called me into his office. His words were these:

"Tony, we have facilities in all our showrooms to offer to our customers tea or coffee. When you are ready to present closing figures this is our company policy. Firstly you tell them you are having a drink and would they prefer tea or coffee. You then return to the closing arena with a 'hot' drink of their choice. They then generally say 'thank you' which puts their mind in a state of acceptance. Then you present your proposal. You will then have at least 10 minutes while they finish their drink to finalise negotiations."

He went on to add that if he saw me present a figure in any other way I would be fired.

This closing method has all my life proved a winner and it does disappoint me even now to visit my clients' sales areas and find salespeople talking about deals worth thousands of pounds in a stand-up situation.

This control element is essential if you are in that type of business but of course not possible if you are selling on buyers' own premises. Ask them for a coffee!!

CLOSE THE SALE

NO. 83

BUYER'S REMORSE CLOSE

Many purchases that people make are important decisions in their lives. Many of them have second thoughts about going ahead even after saying yes to the sale. Many agreements that you now have to offer in sales situations have cancellation clauses built into them. Sometimes it is 24 hours, sometimes 72 hours, and in certain cases as much as 14 days. This of course plants a doubt into the mind of indecisive people and can cause them to change their mind.

On occasions people will sign such documentation and within a few hours are back in or on the telephone wishing to cancel the order.

In such cases you need to explain that very occasionally you have met people like them who have recognised value for money and were positive about the purchase made. Shortly afterwards they may have shared their thoughts with a friend or family member. Those friends or family were possibly well meaning but they may also be a little envious. They certainly were not so well informed and would try to persuade my customers to cancel their purchase. In these instances I have found that after giving the matter a more decisive review my clients would realise that they were correct in their original thoughts. In fact their final agreement with me was a testament to their own good judgement.

CLOSE THE SALE

NO. 84

REJECTION CLOSE

The biggest fear that we have in our industry is rejection! Why, I do not know, for we are in the selling business and we will always have more failure than success.

Empathy is always the best tool to use when someone rejects you along with a little amount of pleading.

When people hit you with rejection, say that you are fully aware that other salespeople will talk to them and all have products that are acceptable. State that you know those salespeople will have financial and persuasive reasons to try and convince them to buy. Of course the buyers can reject all of them if they wish.

What you then need to say is that they cannot say "no" to you because what a rejection means is they are saying "no" to the benefits and customer care that you offer.

Say that you find it very difficult to accept rejection when you know you can provide the product and service they deserve.

Sometimes our clients need help in making their decisions. People cannot often be talked into owning a product they do not want. If their business or their lives will be enhanced by owning your product you must persuade them to have it.

CLOSE THE SALE

NO. 85

MARGIN SHARE CLOSE

Most buyers, contrary to opinion, are not looking for the 'best deal'. If your buyers took your order to three other competitors to obtain a comparison you would have 80% cancelled orders. No! What people want is something they consider fair and reasonable.

Now if you have a 10% mark up on your product and you state you will give 5% discount this is what you are really indicating.

"Mr. Meanor, I have 100% and I am going to keep 95% and give you 5%. Does that sound fair and reasonable?"

Of course it doesn't.

However, if you say:

"Mr. Meanor, we normally give our clients 40% of our margin but today we have in addition a 10% bonus for first time buyers. I will show you what margin we have in the product and you will actually receive 50%. 50/50 sounds fair and reasonable, doesn't it?"

Now does not that sound more acceptable yet it is the same deal as 5% discount.

People generally believe your mark up is bigger than it is. A percentage of margin will always be a more successful close especially if you provide written proof.

CLOSE THE SALE

YOU BECOME A TOP CLOSER

BY WAY OF YOUR RESULTS!

NO. 86

COMPETE CLOSE

If you are in a line of business where people can buy the exact product at different points of sale, this close can be very useful.

Example

When people indicate they are shopping around on price say to them: "Our company policy is to compete with any written quotations within 100 miles of our business. That is fair and reasonable, isn't it?"

Now who is going to travel over 100 miles to buy the same product? Maybe on the internet or mail order if delivery is free of charge!

By using the word 'compete' you are not committing you or your company to anything because you can compete and come second. I know because I have done many times in my chosen sport.

Your buyer however will ponder what is the use of spending time and money visiting other areas to buy the same product. I have used this close hundreds of times successfully.

Every closing situation you are in can teach you something. What works for you, what should be avoided, and what makes you the most money. Detail is paramount. What makes the difference between winning and losing a sale can be small and seemingly insignificant. When it works it is an indescribable feeling of elation. To obtain an order or sale is the second best feeling in the world.

CLOSE THE SALE

NO 87

COMPARISON CLOSE

Some of you may be selling in an industry where it is necessary at times to have to negotiate a trade-in or part-exchange. Examples of this are estate agents, holiday homes, vehicle sales, boats, etc.

When you make an offer on their trade-in you are many times faced with the statement, "I have seen them advertised at a higher price in the newspaper or trade magazines".

For instance, let us use the example of the motor industry. A salesperson says to the buyer: "I will give you £7,000 for your vehicle as a trade-in price". Now the buyer turns around and says "I have seen cars like mine on display and in newspaper adverts at £8,000. Now this looks like, to me anyway, that you are trying to make two profits - one on the new car and one on the used".

A salesperson should reply that, firstly, the asking price/advertised price of a vehicle will probably have discount built into the asking price, for instance when a no-trade-in deal is put forward that may be a reserve of around £300. Secondly, reconditioning and warranty on the vehicle on average would be around £350. Thirdly, with the remaining £350 the dealer would need to pay V.A.T. of 17Ü% (U.K. only) on that gross profit. So all in all the dealer would only be realising a profit of around £280 on an £8,000 asking price, 4%, having given £7,000 for the trade-in. "That is fair and reasonable, isn't it?"

<u>CLOSE THE SALE</u>

NO. 88

DISCOUNT v SERVICE CLOSE

When you are faced with an objection such as "Your competitor will provide the goods at below cost" try not to end up in a price war.

State that you have been in selling for a number of years and that people predominantly look for three benefits when they spend their money. They want the lowest price, the best service and top quality goods. Explain that no company can genuinely offer all three. They certainly cannot offer top quality goods and the best service at the lowest price. Ask them which of those three they would rather lose; top quality, best service or lowest price?

Many of them will reply that the customer care/after sales and quality of goods are the biggest concern which overcomes the price difference!

Go over all the back-up that your company provides and indicate how much you invest in customer care to build long term relationships.

Not all companies will accept a lower offer so you cannot expect to win at all times. If you do lose out put the buyer onto a short and long term follow-up system and write a "thank you" letter for the business opportunity.

No doubt if they go for the cheapest option they will certainly not get 100% after sales care. Next time they may be calling direct to you and appreciate that it is a tough decision to make - discount v service.

CLOSE THE SALE

NO. 89

BREAK TIME CLOSE

Many of you will be selling by having to visit buyers at their premises. Some of you will have to do your sales pitch in front of one - six people presenting your company's product.

When arranging your meeting always make sure that you have established the time you will be presenting to your client, i.e. 15 minute presentation, 15 minutes for questions. This way the buyers do not have to wonder whether you will be finished before the 10.00 p.m. news.

Beware of mobile phones (especially your own) interrupting during meetings. Remember if someone has to leave your presentation and then return it may take them up to 10 minutes to be back at the same level of concentration.

If you are selling involved technology, double-glazed windows or complicated insurance policies, you will of course need to book a longer presentation time.

I once had a salesperson make an appointment at my home to talk about one double-glazed window. His telephone call said he would 'pop' round for a chat. On arriving he then entered my house and said his presentation (with visuals) would take about two - three hours and was glad we were both there. Five minutes later I was gone and he sold to my wife (I had made other plans for the evening). So always stipulate your expected presentation time before arrival. A break time close is where you feel the need to break up the meeting for individual discussions with key personnel to cement the close.

CLOSE THE SALE

NO. 90

RESALE VALUE CLOSE

When a buyer purchases a product, in some instances it can increase in value. Houses, watches, diamonds, paintings and antique furniture are just a few examples. This helps you enormously when gaining commitment.

Some 25 years ago I was furthering my sales career in the Far East market. One day I visited a jeweller in Hong Kong with the intention of purchasing a watch for around 1,000 Hong Kong dollars (around £100 sterling). Through my own ego and being served by an excellent Chinese salesman I bought a Cartier watch which cost me around 6,000 Hong Kong dollars - this was six times more than I had hoped to spend. Why did I buy? Because the salesman took the time to explain to me that the watch must be insured (more outlay) but would increase in value year by year. Today that watch is worth around 30,000 Hong Kong dollars, some 500% increase in value.

If you are selling anything that will increase or hold its value, maybe even devalue very little, this is an area for you to major in in your closing techniques.

You know that your key to success is people and that people in general do not like to waste money. They like to invest it. Much easier for you to close by talking increased value to eliminate that fear of loss that goes with spending money.

CLOSE THE SALE

YOU CANNOT BE A GREAT CLOSER WITHOUT BEING A GREAT QUALIFIER!

NO. 91

CREDIT NOTE CLOSE

When you are selling a product of a medium to large amount this close can be very effective. Not only does it secure the sale but also gains business for the future.

Should you be, for example, £300 apart at the final stages but are selling a product with margins in excess of £1,000 you say something like this:

"Mrs. Robinson, you are at present £300 apart from owning this unique piece of antique furniture. May I make a proposal - if I can persuade my manager to give you a £300 credit note we could solve the problem. It would be valid for three years against the purchase of any other item in our store over the retail value of £2,000. Your home has already many beautiful pieces of furniture which you have purchased from us. I am sure the credit note will be of future use. I will see if I can gain approval before we go any further, okay?"

You see even antique dealers have to keep up with the modern world to stay in business.

It is a great face saving close and of course it is most certain that Mrs. Robinson will be back to use the £300 voucher in the future. It is a good idea to write on the credit note that it must be produced prior to any future negotiations.

CLOSE THE SALE

NO. 92

PAYMENT SAVING CLOSE

There is a saying in our industry: "Successful salespeople are just lucky! Ask any failure". Now the only way you obtain full profit in a sale is to ask for it. So any closing tip that helps you achieve that should be carefully studied and put into practice. If buyers are updating a currently owned product talk to them about upgrading which is what everyone on this planet seems to want to do - improve their way of life. You close the sale when the prospect is ready not when you are ready.

A payment saving close can be used when the prospect currently owns a product on finance terms and is looking for a later model. If you are £200 apart in your negotiations the face saving close goes something like this.

"Mr. Gullible, at present you are paying £182 per month for your current model. If you choose our product on the recommended payments you will obtain a cash flow benefit. We already have your settlement figure but your first payment on the new product will not be due for five weeks. This means where you have paid £182 per month for the last three years a saving will be made for one month! Now we are £200 away from an agreement which I cannot move on. If you take into account the £182 saving I will be able to concede a further £18 to round it off."

CLOSE THE SALE

NO. 93

SELL YOURSELF CLOSE

It is one of the oldest known facts in our profession that you sell yourself first. If someone likes you they will probably buy from you. The golden rules to remember when selling yourself are:

- Learn to remember names. A person's name is important to them.
- Give your buyer the facts - a bit more but no less.
- Be a comfortable person to be with.
- Offer convincing evidence to back up your statements.
- Never act as if you are suffering from stress.
- Talk at a similar speed to your buyer.
- Do not be egotistical. Be as humble as your job allows.
- Draw your buyers into your presentation.
- Be interesting so that people are not looking for the door marked exit.
- Ensure your sales process is logical.
- Try to eliminate any character qualities that you know irritate or annoy people.
- Stick to low-pressure psychological methods of selling.
- Remember most misunderstandings are caused by lack of understanding.
- Ask buyers for their opinion and listen.

- Search for the good points in buyers.
- Choose the right time to stress quality.
- Deal with objections in a non-confrontational manner.
- Avoid using superlatives that you cannot prove.
- Ensure your meeting and greeting wins immediate attention.
- Never miss an opportunity to congratulate or sympathise when called for.
- Make buyers aware of your benefits.
- Build up your sales process to a final act of closing.
- Convince your buyers they need your product from yourself.
- Remember the more people that like you the more money you will earn.

CLOSE THE SALE

NO. 94

"DO NOT" CLOSE

A 'do not' list to sell yourself to the close.

- Do not dress in bad taste. Try to dress to blend with your buyers.
- Do not treat prospects as a waste of time.
- Do not ignore buyers even when you are busy. At least acknowledge them.
- Do not be unfriendly towards prospects as they represent profit.
- Do not be rude to your clients.
- Do not be over-familiar.
- Do not be offhand.
- Do not talk too glibly, which will make the buyer feel that you lack sincerity.
- Do not show little or no interest in your client's business.
- Do not smoke in front of clients.
- Do not make false claims regarding your product.
- Do not criticise your buyer's current product.
- Do not make tactless remarks.
- Do not apologise for the price of your product.
- Do not point out possible weaknesses of your product.
- Do not involve 'trade jargon' in talking with clients.

- Do not offer the buyers unasked for discount.
- Do not be too rigid when negotiating.
- Do not pretend to know the answer to a question when you don't.
- Do not set out to impress yourself and your colleagues before you have impressed the buyer.
- Do not exaggerate the truth.
- Do not drink port after champagne - just checking!

Remember that many people see modesty as a sign of strength, knowledge, confidence and integrity. They would also dismiss any over-brashness as a person who cannot be trusted.

<u>**CLOSE THE SALE**</u>

NO. 95

TWO UP AND ONE DOWN CLOSE

It is hard to say how much knowledge you need to close competently. You as an individual will know what techniques you need for the product you are selling. Do not forget to try to adapt the methods to suit your needs, and remember nothing works all the time. If I could show you one close that had a 100% success rate I would not be sitting here day after day writing this book. Experience or lack of it will dictate your actions.

A two up and one down close is where you are in a closing situation where a lot of bargaining visually takes place. Your concessions may be in most cases money but also accessories, add-ons, warranties, preparation or delivery dates may be part of the negotiation process. When you start to propose figures it may be that you are working through underwritten or head office/management instructions.

Start by giving your first proposal and try to close using any of the ideas put forward in this book. If that first figure fails then you come back with an increased offer. You then try to close the sale. Now here is the rub. Your third offer should be slightly less than the second stating that your management feel the previous offer was too high. On noticing that the buyer looks a little confused with the proceedings you say, "My own feeling is that our company should honour the previous offer. If I can make them realise the importance of the agreement and confirm the last price can I have your business?"

CLOSE THE SALE

EVERYBODY CAN GET IT RIGHT -

ONE DAY AT A TIME!

NO. 96

EXTENDED MONTHLY PAYMENT CLOSE

Extended monthly payments is when you close by fixing the monthly payments to suit the buyer's budget.

If you ask them what weekly figure they have in mind they will give you a figure. It is possible that the figure that is within their proposed budget is not sufficient for you to conclude the deal. What you have to do then is keep extending the monthly payments by periods of six months until it does suit their requested figures.

As long as you have a good knowledge of your product and service and appear confident in your presentation you will be seen as a person trying to help them.

When negotiating finance terms, people sometimes mention that the payments are outside their budget because they have other outstanding commitments such as mortgage, credit card payments and personal or car loans. Do not miss an opportunity to suggest a consolidation of finances which would help them achieve the required budgetary figure to purchase your product. By borrowing more from yourselves and paying off one or two smaller loans or credit cards, you can:

1) Supply your product.

2) Help them reduce monthly outgoings.

3) Increase your finance commission.

<u>CLOSE THE SALE</u>

NO. 97

PERCENTAGE OF MARKET CLOSE

When I first went to sell in the United States of America my boss took me in the office on the first day and said, "Tony, I believe that a good salesperson closes on average around the fifth close. Now different closes work with different people so study all you can about the art of persuasion". I remember walking out of his office as a 26 year old with six years' selling experience calculating that I only knew three closing techniques. I vowed then to spend the rest of my career learning as much as I could about this skill.

A percentage of market close can be used where you are selling a product which is a market leader.

Example

I was working recently with a sales team in the United Kingdom who sold Ford motor cars. In the U.K. Ford have around 20% of the market share. I explained to the team the importance of using this close.

I said, say to a buyer at the closing stages, "Mr. Stillman, in this country thousands and thousands of motor cars are bought every single day. In reality people can choose from over a thousand models from vehicles being built in the Far East, U.S.A., Europe and including the United Kingdom. A simple fact is though, that every day when these people go out to reward themselves with a new car one out of five still choose a Ford motor car - an impressive figure, don't you agree?"

CLOSE THE SALE

NO. 98

"PIECE OF CAKE" CLOSE

When my son and daughter were very young they were like all children when it came to cake or ice cream. When it was put on the table in front of them, both Matthew and Sarah would want 'the lion's share' of the scrumptious food. After a few months of watching my wife, Pat, suffer a few tantrums from the kids, I made a suggestion.

"In future one of you can cut the cake or ice cream and the other chooses which piece they want!" All agreed this was a fair and reasonable way to behave and on most occasions it worked very well. My wife and I did try it with the wine at dinner when the children were in bed but, after a couple of glasses, you tended to forget where you started.

This 'piece of cake' close works very well in a selling situation where you have to give between 40% and 80% of your own margin away to compete with your competitors' prices. A sales process must take into account the fact that buyers are looking for an offer that appears to be fair and reasonable. It also must be presented correctly with documentary evidence to work for you and also fit into the customer's requirements. So how do we use this persuasive closing statement?

"Mr. Wong, you can see by my documentation that we have £740 margin in our product. If I divide that figure into two and let you choose, I am sure you will agree that is fair and reasonable, isn't it?"

CLOSE THE SALE

NO. 99

PRICE JUSTIFICATION CLOSE

Handling price objections is the most frequent and most difficult area to cope with. Value for money is what all buyers are looking for. Most people have at least five ways of avoiding the close so if you, as a salesperson, only know two or three ways to close, you will run out of closing ideas long before they run out of "I'll think about it" material.

Always describe price alongside benefits then it will appear as value for money. Avoid price barriers such as quoting £10,000 instead of £9,950; £19,500 sounds a lot less than £20,000. Amortise your prices down to weekly or daily figures such as £49 per week instead of £211 per month. Always avoid round figures as these never appear to be your best price.

Negotiating is the process of closing a sale and agreeing the terms on which it is arranged. It is an important business skill. Good negotiators are always in a strong position to impress people and to conclude a good deal.

You always learn interesting things when you carry out customer surveys for major companies. I conducted one recently where I asked people why they had not bought the product they had looked at. Of course the most common answer was that they were never asked. A salesperson had done everything right but did not ask them for a commitment or to part with their money, so they didn't.

Treat all price objections as steps on the ladder to the sale, overcome them by professional price justification methods and ask for the order!

CLOSE THE SALE

NO. 100

THANK YOU CARD CLOSE

Let me tell you about Darren Hannah. He had a promising career as a professional soccer player ruined by injury. I met Darren when he was 19 and had joined a motor company with whom I was involved in training and coaching.

Darren had never sold motor cars before but was determined to make up for the loss of high earnings he would have made as a soccer player.

Every few weeks I would visit the dealership and go through my learning programme with all the staff including Darren.

Now Darren was very soon top man and still is today nearly five years later. Other sales-people have joined and most of them left for various reasons. Darren has sold over 400 cars every year while the average is around 200. He has gained much of the financial security he craved and last time I was there he was driving around in the latest Porsche and has his own home and family. Darren is still only 25 years old.

'Thank you card' close is one I put forward to Darren on one of my first training courses. I told him that every time a customer sent him a thank you card to put it on display on his desk so customers could read the kind comments. Today Darren has a stand next to his desk with over 100 current thank you cards on display. Incidentally, the other salespeople have still not seen the benefit! When Darren presents his proposal to his customers he will point out his card display and say, "those are my happy clients".

CLOSE THE SALE

A LOSER NEVER WINS

AND

A WINNER NEVER LOSES

ACKNOWLEDGEMENTS

I have always been far too busy in life to be an original thinker. Over the years I have worked with tens of thousands of salespeople all over the globe. Every single skill I possess I have learned from watching listening or reading. I thank all of those people for giving me the profitable ideas that have benefited me during my career.

I would like to thank Sandra Clemens for all the hard work in assisting me with this project.

Finally, I must mention my family who have allowed me the time, space and encouragement to follow an international selling career.